The Cake Parlour
SWEET TABLES
Zoe Clark

D&C
David and Charles
www.rucraft.co.uk

CONTENTS

Sweet table sensation!

After the craze for cupcake and mini cake towers of the past few years, we now have a new sweet sensation that has taken the celebration scene by storm - bring on the sweet table! Much more than just a fancily displayed, elaborate cake centrepiece, this is a complete collection of coordinating cakes and confectionery themed around an event. This exciting creative development was pioneered in the USA, notably through the inspirational schemes of Martha Stewart and more recently Amy Atlas.

Sweet tables can make a stunning impact, as you'll see from the designs in this book, and are certain to add oodles of style to any special occasion and wow your guests. In fact, they can create a whole atmosphere and set just the right mood so that the event is on course for success right from the start. Sweet tables can also help in practical terms, as they're an ideal way to cater for all tastes and can act as a dessert buffet, where people can help themselves rather than being served.

Here, I have designed six unique and distinctively styled sweet tables, one specifically for the festive season and another for new baby celebrations, but the remainder can be tailored to a variety of occasions, from romantic weddings and Valentine's to special birthday parties and sophisticated soirées. The design based on the branding of my own shop; The Cake Parlour, is a perfect example of a scheme that can be adopted or adapted for all kinds of get-togethers, elevating them into classy, elegant events.

Each scheme features a show-stopping centrepiece cake, with detailed instructions and photos to guide you in re-creating it, and an accompanying range of confections, including cookies and cupcakes, macaroons and mini cakes – and more. A separate reference section gives you lots of failsafe recipes for cakes, fillings and coverings, as well as explanations and demonstrations of the baking, covering and decorating techniques involved.

The key to a successful sweet table is in creating a harmonious display, and both colour and pattern are essential in linking the various elements together. These can be personalized and themed with the particular event, such as coordinating with bespoke wedding stationery – the confectionery labels or signs, for example, could easily be designed to match. But you also need to think about the overall structure and composition, using risers and stands to create varying heights and different containers to give contrasting shapes. Choosing the appropriate table and covering is clearly crucial too, and texture can play a part here as well as colour. A suitable backdrop can also greatly enhance a sweet scene and bring it added drama.

Above all, styling your own sweet tables can be great fun, as it offers you the chance to work creatively with friends and family both in the planning and the practice, and I hope this book gives you all the know-how you need – plus the all-important inspiration!

The Candy COLLECTION

Invite your guests to step into your own private candy store and delight
in the dazzling colours and sweet sensations of yesteryear.

Jelly Beans

Lollipops

Twisters

Sweetie Cookies

Cake Pops

Rainbow Twists

Millions

Mini Cakes

Whirly Pops

Mini Cupcakes

Fondant Fancies

Candy stack spectacular

This design undoubtedly has the wow factor, but it actually involves no sugarcraft at all beyond the icing of the cake. To achieve a smart, stylish result, I have kept to one dominant colour. If the cake is too big for the number of guests, just use fake tiers top and bottom to retain the full impact.

Materials

One 13cm (5in) and one 18cm (7in) round cake, 9cm (3½in) deep, prepared and iced in white sugarpaste (rolled fondant) at least 12-24 hours in advance (see Recipes and Techniques)

One 23cm (9in) round cake, 13cm (5in) deep, prepared and iced in white sugarpaste at least 12-24 hours in advance (see Recipes and Techniques)

One 28cm (11in) round cake dummy, 5cm (2in) deep, iced in white sugarpaste at least 12-24 hours in advance, and one 35.5cm (14in) round cake board, covered in white sugarpaste (see Baking and Covering Techniques: Icing Cake Boards and Dummies)

¼ quantity royal icing (see Decorating Techniques: Royal Icing)

SWEETS 16 orange Haribo Rotella fruit wheels, 12-14 Twizzlers Strawberry Twists, about 45 red Skittles, about 65 Fruit Flavour Candy Planks, 9 lollipops 4cm (1½in) round, Cinnamon Hearts to fill sundae dish

Equipment

8 hollow pieces of dowel (if using all real cakes - 4 for bottom tier, 3 for middle tier, 1 for top tier), cut to size (see Baking and Covering Techniques: Assembling Tiered Cakes)

RIBBON 1.5cm (⅝in) bright pink, pink, yellow, red satin

Small paper piping (pastry) bag (see Decorating Techniques: Making a Piping Bag)

Glass sundae dish

Basic equipment (see Tools and Equipment)

If you can't find the candy specified or prefer other sweets, make your own choice in two or three colours.

Candies

a

b

c

Start by assembling and sorting all the sweets you need for the cake. (a)

To assemble the cake, begin by dowelling and assembling the 28cm (11in) cake dummy on the base board (see Baking and Covering Techniques: Assembling Tiered Cakes). Then set up the three tiers descending in size on top, dowelling the cakes as you go. You will also need to insert one dowel into the top tier if you are placing a heavy sundae dish on top, especially if the cake inside is a sponge cake. Secure the bright pink ribbon around the top tier and the pink ribbon around the 23cm (9in) tier (see Baking and Covering Techniques: Securing Ribbon Around Cakes and Boards).

For the top tier, fill a small piping bag (without a piping tube/tip) with the royal icing. Use it to stick the Rotellas around the cake just above the ribbon.

For the 18cm (7in) tier, (b) cut one of the Strawberry Twists about 7.5cm (3in) long and use this to measure and cut the rest of the Twists to go round the tier. Squeeze a tiny amount of royal icing down the sweets and stick them around the cake, extending from the base upwards, positioning them side by side close together. Use small dots of royal icing to stick the red Skittles around the cake above the Strawberry Twists.

For the bottom tier, stick the Planks around the cake in the same way as for the Strawberry Twists.

For the 23cm (9in) tier, (c) tie a length of yellow ribbon in a bow at the top of each lollipop stick. Trim the ends neatly and at an angle. Dab some royal icing onto the back of the candy discs and stick the lollipops to the cake. The sticks can rest on the ledge of the tier below, but the weight should be taken at the top of the lollipops so that the sticks don't sink into the icing. Therefore, you may need to hold the lollipops in place for a few seconds until they are stuck in place securely.

To finish, secure the red ribbon around the base board. Once the cake is in place on the table, fill the sundae dish with Cinnamon Hearts and place it on top of the cake. Use a small amount of royal icing to stick it down if you like.

To add interest to your candy table, display any leftover sweets and extra eye-catching candy in coordinating colours in a mix of different sized and shaped glass display jars.

Zingy mini cupcakes

These bright little cakes are so simple to create, yet they bring a real punch to the table with their contrasting blue sprinkles. You could even use popping candy for added excitement! For an extra flavour infusion, 'inject' your sponge with delicious raspberry jam (see Baking and Covering Techniques: Preparing and Icing Cupcakes).

YOU'LL ALSO NEED
Lemon-flavoured mini cupcakes, baked in silver foil mini cupcake cases (liners) (see Baking and Covering Techniques: Baking Cupcakes)

Yellow-coloured lemon-flavoured buttercream (see Fillings and Coverings)

Pearlescent turquoise Sparkling Sugar Crystals

Medium-large disposable plastic piping (pastry) bag

1cm (⅜in) plain piping tube (tip)

One Fit the plastic piping bag with the piping tube and fill the bag with the yellow-coloured lemon-flavoured buttercream. Pipe a buttercream kiss onto each cupcake (see Baking and Covering Techniques: Preparing and Icing Cupcakes).

Two Sprinkle the centre of each freshly piped buttercream kiss with the sugar crystals.

As these cakes are so small, bake and decorate them as near to serving time as possible so that they don't dry out.

Mini dizzy delights

The classic candy colour combination of red and white is used for this dynamic display of mini cakes, but choose any strong colour to suit your scheme.

YOU'LL ALSO NEED
5cm (2in) round mini cakes, flavour of choice, prepared and iced in white sugarpaste (rolled fondant) (see Baking and Covering Techniques: Mini Cakes)

Red Haribo Rotella fruit wheels

Strawberry sherbet, to display (optional)

1.5cm (⅝in) orange satin ribbon

One Wrap the orange ribbon around the base of each cake and secure in place with a dot of royal icing.

Two Stick a red Rotella on top of each cake in the centre. Display the cakes on a white plate covered with a layer of strawberry sherbet to match the colour of the Rotellas if you like.

Stripy sweetie cookies

For a taste of nostalgia, create these charming cookies shaped and iced to mimic old-fashioned boiled sweets in traditional candy-stripe wrappers.

One For the purple striped sweets, fill a small paper piping (pastry) bag fitted with a no. 1 piping tube with purple royal icing. Start by piping a line around the outside edge either side of the cookies, then pipe a line down the centre and finally two lines either side of the central line (see Decorating Techniques: Piping with Royal Icing). Pipe a little dot at the end of each line.

Two Fill another piping bag fitted with the no. 1 piping tube with white royal icing and pipe around the outside edge of the ends of each cookie. Pipe a crease line from each purple dot to the piped edge of the ends of the cookies.

Three For the green striped sweets, repeat the process above using green royal icing.

YOU'LL ALSO NEED
Wrapped boiled sweet (hard candy)-shaped vanilla-flavoured cookies, iced with white royal icing (see Baking and Covering Techniques: Baking Cookies and Decorating Techniques: Royal-Iced Cookies)

ROYAL ICING purple and green

No. 1 piping tube (tip)

15

Rocking red lollipops

These cake pops look just like hard candy lollipops with their jolly red coating. You could wrap them in cellophane tied with ribbon and give to your guests to take away.

YOU'LL ALSO NEED
Uncoated cake pops, chilled
(see Baking and Covering Techniques:
Cake Pops)

Red Candy Melts

Pearlescent Pink
Sparkling Sugar Crystals

One Melt the Candy Melts as instructed in the section on Cake Pops (see Baking and Covering Techniques). Dip the cake pops into the melted candy one at a time.

Two Transfer to a sheet of baking (parchment) paper and immediately sprinkle each one with the pink sugar crystals. Leave to dry.

Candy crunch fab fancies

Brightly coloured sweets make an instant, fun topping for plain white fondant fancies in coordinating foil cases and also give them an extra textural dimension.

Following the instructions in Fondant Fancies (see Baking and Covering Techniques), once you have dipped the sponge squares one at a time into the warmed white fondant, immediately sprinkle them with the green and blue sweets (candies) so that they stick before the fondant dries. Leave to dry.

YOU'LL ALSO NEED
Fondant fancies, filling of choice, dipped in white fondant and set in blue foil cases (liners) (see Baking and Covering Techniques: Fondant Fancies)

Green Skittles and blue Millions

A romance OF RUFFLES

Craft a sophisticated collection of sensuous desserts softly textured
with piped swirls, frills and ruffles in dreamy, muted tones.

Fantasy frills

This fabulous trio of celebration cakes is a study in texture and tone, featuring the use of buttercream as the decorating medium rather than the usual smooth sugarpaste. The three distinct designs are created using the same basic technique and piping tube but worked in slightly different ways and tones. The ruffled tiers are contrasted with plain tiers to accentuate the textural effects.

Materials – For the four-tier cake

One 13cm (5in) and one 20cm (8in) round cake, 9cm (3½in) deep, layered, filled with filling of choice and coated with buttercream (see Recipes and Techniques)

One 15cm (6in) and one 25cm (10in) round cake, 13cm (5in) deep, layered with four layers of sponge, filled and coated with buttercream (see Recipes and Techniques)

One 33cm (13in) round cake board, covered with ivory sugarpaste (rolled fondant) (see Baking and Covering Techniques: Icing Cake Boards and Dummies)

1.5kg (3lb 5oz) vanilla-flavoured buttercream or Swiss meringue buttercream (see Fillings and Coverings)

A little royal icing (see Decorating Techniques: Royal Icing)

Non-toxic roses (David Austin Roses), to decorate (optional)

Equipment

Hollow pieces of dowel, cut to size (see Baking and Covering Techniques: Assembling Tiered Cakes)

Cake dummy, cake stand or heavy-duty turntable

Large disposable plastic piping (pastry) bags

Petal piping tube (tip) no. 103

RIBBON 1.5cm (⅝in) ivory, coffee, peach satin

Flower picks (optional)

Basic equipment (see Tools and Equipment)

Unless you have access to refrigerated transport on the day, assemble the upper tiers of the four-tier cake on site.

Four-tier

Before you begin, make sure the cakes have been well chilled in the fridge so that they are easier to handle.

For the four-tier cake

Start by coating the 13cm (5in) and 20cm (8in) tiers in a second coat of buttercream with a palette knife. Be fairly generous with the buttercream, especially around the sides of the cakes, so that you can't see the cake through it. Try to be as neat as possible and to create sharp, clean edges around the top. Return the cakes to the fridge to chill for about 20 minutes or so.

To assemble the cake, dowel the 25cm (10in) tier (see Baking and Covering Techniques: Assembling Tiered Cakes) and set it up on the sugarpaste-covered cake board, securing it in place with some royal icing. As there is no sugarpaste covering on the cake, this can be a little messy.

Next dowel the 20cm (8in) cake and very carefully stick it on top of the 25cm (10in) tier, taking care not to damage the neat buttercream around the sides.

Then dowel the 15cm (6in) tier and place it on top of the 20cm (8in) cake. Lastly, assemble the 13cm (5in) tier on top of the 15cm (6in) tier, taking care not to mark the buttercream.

Freeze the two plain tiers briefly before stacking so that the buttercream is really hard and less likely to get damaged.

For the piping, set the cake on a cake dummy, cake stand or heavy-duty turntable to make it easier to turn the cake. Cut a hole in the end of a disposable plastic piping bag and insert the petal piping tube. Fill the bag with some buttercream, but avoid overfilling it, otherwise your hand will begin to ache when you are piping. Work with an amount you feel comfortable with.

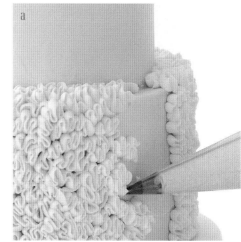

(a) Hold the piping bag so that the hole in the piping tube is perpendicular to the side of the 15cm (6in) cake and the fine end of the tube is facing outwards in order to give the ruffled edge good definition. The bag should be angled almost across the cake in front of you (if you are left-handed, you will be holding the bag to the left of the tube).

Squeeze the buttercream out, moving the piping tube up and down and in a wavy fashion, at the same time keeping the wider end of the tube very close to the cake. Working from the left and following the cake round to the right, if you are right-handed, go back and forth randomly over the surface of the cake to create a wiggly, uneven ruffled effect. Turn the sharp end of the tube upwards around the top edge of the cake so that the ruffled edge follows the shape of the cake.

Continue around the cake until the tier is covered in ruffles, refilling the piping bag when you start to run out of buttercream. If the buttercream at the end of your bag starts to melt with the heat from your hand, squeeze it out and use a fresh batch.

(b) Repeat the piping process around the 25cm (10in) tier.

Finish by securing the ivory ribbon around the cake board (c) (see Baking and Covering Techniques: Securing Ribbon Around Cakes and Boards). Decorate the top of the cake and the bottom tier with non-toxic roses if you like. Insert the stems into flower picks to push into the cake and hold in place.

Practise the piping technique on a test surface to gain your confidence before working on the cake itself.

Two-tier

Materials – For the two-tier cake

One 13cm (5in) round cake, 9cm (3½in) deep, and one 18cm (7in) round cake, 13cm (5in) deep, layered, filled with filling of choice and coated with coffee-flavoured or coffee-coloured buttercream (see Fillings and Coverings)

One 25cm (10in) round cake board, covered with coffee-coloured sugarpaste (rolled fondant) (see Baking and Covering Techniques: Icing Cake Boards and Dummies)

750g (1lb 10oz) coffee-flavoured or coffee-coloured vanilla-flavoured buttercream or Swiss meringue buttercream (see Fillings and Coverings)

A little royal icing (see Decorating Techniques: Royal Icing)

Non-toxic roses (David Austin Roses), to decorate (optional)

For the two-tier cake

Start by applying a neat, generous second coat of coffee-flavoured or coffee-coloured buttercream to the top tier of the cake and return it to the fridge for 20 minutes or so until set firm.

To assemble the cake, dowel the 18cm (7in) tier and stick it onto the coffee-coloured iced cake board with royal icing (see Baking and Covering Techniques: Assembling Tiered Cakes). Stack the 13cm (5in) tier on top.

For the piping, set the cake on a cake dummy, cake stand or heavy-duty turntable to make it easier to turn the cake. Cut a hole in the end of a disposable plastic piping bag and insert the petal piping tube. Fill the bag with some of the coffee buttercream without overfilling it.

a

(a) Hold the bag at an approximately 45-degree angle to the cake with the piping tube perpendicular to the cake, the fine end of the tube facing outwards and the wider end barely touching the side. Working from the bottom of the cake upwards, move the tube from side to side, squeezing out the buttercream as you go. The width of the ruffles is about 2.5cm (1in). Stop when you get to the top edge. Repeat around the tier until it is covered with columns of ruffles.

Don't feel as though you need to pipe the whole height of the cake in one go – it's fine to stop and then start again if necessary.

(b) Turn the piping tube upwards and away from the top edge of the cake so that the sharp or fine end of the tube is still facing outwards and pipe a ruffled edge along the top edge of the vertical ruffles around the cake – if you are right-handed, you will be working clockwise around the cake. Repeat to pipe another row slightly inside the first row so that the ruffles come up to the base of the top tier.

b

c

(c) Holding the piping bag sideways in front of the base of the top tier with the tip of the tube vertical (the sharp end pointing upwards), pipe a final row of ruffles around the base of the 13cm (5in) cake. This time, work anti(counter)clockwise around the cake if you are right-handed.

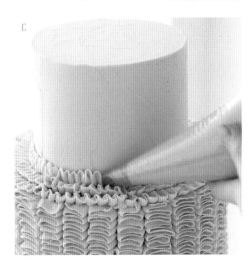

Finish by securing the coffee ribbon around the cake board (see Baking and Covering Techniques: Securing Ribbon Around Cakes and Boards). Decorate the bottom tier with non-toxic roses if you like. Insert the stems into flower picks to push into the cake and hold in place.

Peach cake

Materials – For the peach cake

One 15cm (6in) round cake, 13cm (5in) deep, layered, filled with filling of choice and coated with peach-coloured buttercream (see Recipes and Techniques)

One 20cm (8in) round cake board, covered with peach-coloured sugarpaste (rolled fondant) (see Baking and Covering Techniques: Icing Cake Boards and Dummies)

400g (14oz) peach-coloured vanilla-flavoured buttercream or Swiss meringue buttercream (see Fillings and Coverings)

For the peach cake

For the piping, set the cake on a cake dummy, cake stand or heavy-duty turntable to make it easier to turn the cake. Cut a hole in the end of a disposable plastic piping bag and insert the petal piping tube. Fill the bag with some peach-coloured buttercream without overfilling it.

Hold the piping bag so that the hole in the piping tube is perpendicular to the side of the cake and the fine end of the tube is facing outwards in order to give the ruffled edge good definition (see the Four-Tier Cake). The bag should be angled almost across the cake in front of you (if you are left-handed, you will be holding the bag to the left of the tube).

This time, instead of creating a random ruffled pattern over the cake, move the piping bag up and down to create a single row of ruffles around the cake at a time. Start at the bottom of the cake and work your way upwards. If you are right-handed, work anti(counter)clockwise around the cake.

When you reach the top of the cake, turn the piping tube upwards and outwards, and this time work clockwise around the edge of the cake to create rows of ruffles, continuing the piping into the centre of the top of the cake (see the Two-Tier Cake).

Finish by securing the peach ribbon around the cake board (see Baking and Covering Techniques: Securing Ribbon Around Cakes and Boards).

White chocolate whirls

Quick and easy to make, these inviting bite-size cake balls have a luxurious white chocolate coating that is loosely textured in keeping with the ruffled theme.

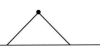

YOU'LL ALSO NEED

Truffle-size cake balls (see Baking and Covering Techniques: Cake Pops)

Tempered white chocolate (see Decorating Techniques: Working with Chocolate)

Cocoa powder (unsweetened cocoa), for dusting

Disposable gloves

Fine sieve (strainer)

One Put on a pair of disposable gloves. Dip the cake balls one at a time into the tempered white chocolate and then roll them in your hands, removing some of the excess chocolate and creating a ruffled, textured surface. Carefully place them on a sheet of baking (parchment) paper and leave to set.

Two Using a fine sieve, sift cocoa over each ball at a time before serving.

Flouncy flower cookies

These simple round cookies are transformed into decadent delights by a frilly, flowery piped royal-icing decoration created using the same petal piping tube as featured in the main cakes. Make a pleasing arrangement of them on a glass cake stand, overlapping them with care.

YOU'LL ALSO NEED

5cm (2in) round cookies (see Baking and Covering Techniques: Baking Cookies)

Pale peach-coloured stiff-peak royal icing (see Decorating Techniques: Royal Icing)

Flower nail

Large pearl dragées (sugar balls)

One Fill a large disposable plastic piping (pastry) bag fitted with the petal piping tube (tip) no. 103 with the peach royal icing. Smear a small amount of icing onto the flower nail and stick a cookie on top. Starting at the outer part of the cookie and holding the piping bag with the sharp or fine end of the piping tube facing outwards, pipe a series of petal shapes in a similar way to piping around the top edge of the bottom tier of the Two-Tier Cake, working in a clockwise circle (if right-handed) around the cookie and turning the nail as you go.

Rather than squeezing continuously, ease off the pressure as you come inwards each time, then squeeze again to make the next petal shape so that it almost looks like it is tucked underneath the previous one.

Two Repeat the process to pipe an inner circle of petal shapes on the cookie.

Three Place a large pearl dragée in the centre of each decorated cookie.

If you don't have a flower nail, you can use a turntable or small cake stand instead to turn the cookies while piping them.

Ruched ribbon cupcakes

These flamboyant cupcakes echo the ruffled look of the big ones, and offer an easier alternative. The decoration makes a nice change from the classic buttercream swirl.

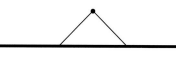

YOU'LL ALSO NEED
Cupcakes, flavour of choice, baked in silver foil cupcake cases (liners) (see Baking and Covering Techniques: Baking Cupcakes)

Turntable

One Fill a large disposable plastic piping (pastry) bag fitted with the petal piping tube (tip) no. 103 with coffee-flavoured or coffee-coloured buttercream and place a cupcake onto a turntable. Holding the piping bag with the sharper edge of the piping tube facing outwards and slightly upwards, pipe a row of ruffles around the outer part of the cupcake in a similar way to piping around the top edge of the bottom tier of the Two-Tier Cake, working in a clockwise direction (if right-handed) around the cupcake and turning the turntable as you go.

Two Pipe another row of ruffles inside and slightly overlapping the outer row, then a small circle of ruffles in the centre to finish.

Tempting twirls of meringue

Soft ivory-coloured meringue is piped into uniform squiggles to create these elegant, crisp confections, adding another interesting textural element to the ruffled theme.

YOU'LL ALSO NEED

Meringue mix, coloured with ivory food colouring (see Baking and Covering Techniques: Meringues)

Large petal piping tube (tip) no. 124

Baking trays (sheets) lined with silicone sheets

One Fill a large disposable plastic piping (pastry) bag fitted with the large petal piping tube with some of the meringue mix. With the wider edge of the tube touching the lined baking tray (sheet) and the sharper end pointing straight up, pipe squiggles by moving the bag from side to side about 2.5cm (1in) wide and stopping when the meringue is about 7.5cm (3in) long. Leave ample space between each piped twirl.

Two Bake the meringues according to the instructions given in Meringues (see Baking and Covering Techniques).

A feast of
ROSES

Celebrate the most romantic day of the year with a sumptuous spread
of rich red and deep pink confections with delectable chocolate accents.

Passion pink
macaroon tower

What better way to woo your true love than with this tower of irresistible pink macaroons piled high on a base of clustered red roses. The blooms are straightforward to create with layers of moulded petals, but they do take time.

Materials

One 25cm (10in) round cake, 10cm (4in) deep, prepared and iced in ruby red sugarpaste (rolled fondant) at least 12-24 hours in advance (see Recipes and Techniques)

One polystyrene cone, 25cm (10in) in diameter and 60cm (23in) high, stuck onto a thin cake board with royal icing, iced in burgundy sugarpaste at least 24 hours in advance (see Baking and Covering Techniques: Icing Cake Boards and Dummies)

Two 35.5cm (14in) round cake boards, stuck together with royal icing, covered with burgundy sugarpaste (see Baking and Covering Techniques: Icing Cake Boards and Dummies)

750g (1lb 10oz) ruby red sugarpaste, 300g (10½oz) ruby red flower (petal/gum) paste and 3 tsp CMC, kneaded together

About 120 deep pink macaroons, filled with ganache (see Baking and Covering Techniques: Macaroons)

75g (2¾oz) plain (semisweet or bittersweet) chocolate or ganache

¼ quantity royal icing (see Decorating Techniques: Royal Icing)

Fuchsia (Squire's Kitchen) edible dust; red (Sugarflair) food colour

Equipment

Plastic sleeve

About 60 cocktail sticks (toothpicks), cut in half

Small paper piping (pastry) bags (see Decorating Techniques: Making a Piping Bag)

4 hollow pieces of dowel, cut to size, if using real cake (see Baking and Covering Techniques: Assembling Tiered Cakes)

RIBBON 1.5cm (⅝in) burgundy satin, 7cm (2¾in) chocolate brown double-faced satin

Basic equipment (see Tools and Equipment)

You can use a dummy rather than a real 25cm (10in) cake, in which case you don't need to stick the cone to a thin board.

Roses

Start by making the roses. You will need about 125 in total, two-thirds large (about 83) and one-third small (about 42) (or simply make the base shallower to reduce the amount). Once you have kneaded together the red sugarpaste, flower paste and CMC, keep it in a plastic bag to prevent it from drying out.

(a) Roll about 75g (2¾oz) of the paste into a long, thin sausage shape about 1cm (⅜in) in diameter and cut into marble-size pieces, weighing about 7g (⅛oz) each. You will need nine pieces per large rose.

(b) Lightly grease the plastic sleeve with white vegetable fat (shortening) to prevent the paste from sticking. Roll one piece of cut paste into a smaller sausage and the rest into balls. Place all the pieces between the plastic sleeve and press down on each piece slightly to flatten it. Press down again more along one side, leaving the other side fairly thick.

(c) and (d) Take the small sausage shape first and roll one end inwards to make the centre of the rose. Wrap three petals around the centre roll so that they overlap one another. Squeeze the base of the rose slightly if necessary to keep the rose together.

If the paste is too soft or sticky, leave it for 10 minutes for the CMC to develop and harden the paste. If it's still too sticky, knead in a little more CMC.

(e) and (f) Next wrap the outer five petals around the three-petal layer, again tucking each petal into one another. Squeeze the rose at the base to hold all the petals in place.

(g) and (h) Ease back the petals of the outer layer so that they look more like real rose petals. Continue squeezing the base of the rose and then pull away the excess paste. Set the rose aside on a tray lined with a sheet of baking (parchment) paper.

To make the small roses, repeat the process used for the large roses but without adding the five petals for the outer layer. Once the three petals are attached around the centre of the rose, simply peel them back as before and then pull away the excess paste from the base.

You can make the roses well in advance and store them in a box (not an airtight container) in a cool, dry place.

Assembly

To create the macaroon cone, start by mounting the first row of macaroons onto the cone. To do this, first push the blunt cut end of a cocktail stick into the cone. Melt some chocolate and place in a small paper piping bag (without a piping tube/tip). Use a minimal amount of the melted chocolate to secure the stick in place on the cone, then push the macaroon onto the pointed end of the stick. Alternatively, you could use ganache.

Stick the 25cm (10in) cake onto the iced board with royal icing. Dowel the cake (if using a real cake) and assemble the cone on top, securing it in place with royal icing (see Baking and Covering Techniques: Assembling Tiered Cakes).

(a) Continue sticking the macaroons onto the cone, working your way up row by row. Your macaroons will probably vary slightly in size, so try to arrange them around the cake neatly, avoiding creating any gaps.

(b) Dust the roses with the fuchsia edible dust.

(c) Cut off the base of each rose with a small, sharp knife so that it sits flat. Colour some royal icing deep red with the red food colouring (see Decorating Techniques: Colouring Icings) and fill a small paper piping bag with it (without a piping tube/tip). Starting at the base, stick the roses onto the 25cm (10in) cake with the icing, placing them close together. Continue until the cake is completely covered, adding roses right up under the macaroons to hide the gap between the cone and the cake.

To finish, secure the burgundy ribbon around the edge of the cake base (see Baking and Covering Techniques: Securing Ribbon Around Cakes and Boards). Tie a length of the chocolate brown double-faced satin ribbon in a bow. Stick the bow onto the cone near the top with a small amount of royal icing, or secure in place with a cocktail stick.

Rose petal confetti cupcakes

These classy chocolate cupcakes, scattered confetti style with realistic-looking rose petals, are incredibly easy to whip up, and appeal to the heart and taste buds alike.

YOU'LL ALSO NEED

Chocolate cupcakes, baked in brown foil cupcake cases (liners), each topped with a ganache kiss piped with a plain piping tube (tip) (see Baking and Covering Techniques: Baking Cupcakes and Preparing and Icing Cupcakes)

ROSE-PETAL CUTTERS 4cm (1½in), 4.5cm (1¾in) in length

Foam pad

Ball tool

Crumpled foil

One Thinly roll out some ruby red flower (petal/gum) paste and cut out petals using the cutters. Place the petals on a foam pad and soften the edges with a ball tool. Peel back the top of the petal slightly on both sides using a cocktail stick (toothpick) to help you and set aside to dry in a petal-like position on crumpled foil.

Two Dust the rose petals with the fuchsia edible dust, as used in the main cake, and position them randomly on the cupcakes.

Romancing raspberry truffles

No Valentine dessert spread is complete without a bowl of indulgent dark chocolate truffles. These are finished off in style with a sprinkling of crystallized raspberries.

YOU'LL ALSO NEED

Soft ganache, flavoured with raspberry liqueur if you like (see Fillings and Coverings)

Hollow plain (semisweet or bittersweet) chocolate truffle shells

Tempered plain (semisweet or bittersweet) chocolate (see Decorating Techniques: Working with Chocolate)

Crystallized raspberries

Disposable plastic piping (pastry) bag

Dipping forks

One Fill the piping bag with the soft ganache, snip a small hole in the end and squeeze it into the hollow truffle shells, making sure that the shells are completely filled without leaving any air pockets (see Decorating Techniques: Working with Chocolate). Dip a small palette knife into some tempered plain chocolate and dab it over the holes of the shells to seal. Leave to set.

Two Using one or two dipping forks, dip the truffles one at a time into the bowl of tempered chocolate, lift out and allow the excess chocolate to drip off before transferring to a sheet of baking (parchment) paper (see Decorating Techniques: Working with Chocolate). Sprinkle a few flakes of crystallized raspberries on the top of each truffle before the chocolate sets. Leave the truffles on the paper to set completely.

Chocolate-wrapped rose raptures

A taste of chocoholic heaven, these stylistic mini cakes are encased in a sleek, shiny chocolate collar and crowned with a single perfect red rose. Handle the cakes carefully, ideally wearing special cotton gloves, so that you don't leave finger marks on the glossy chocolate.

YOU'LL ALSO NEED

5cm (2in) round chocolate mini cakes, covered with ganache (see Baking and Covering Techniques: Mini Cakes)

Tempered plain (semisweet or bittersweet) chocolate (see Decorating Techniques: Working with Chocolate)

6cm (2½in) wide acetate

Medium cranked palette knife

One Measure the circumference of one of your mini cakes. Stand all the cakes on a sheet of baking (parchment) paper. Cut pieces of acetate about 1cm (⅜in) longer than the cake circumference – this should be approximately 19cm (7½in).

Two Lay the pieces of acetate out on a flat surface. Working on three or four pieces at a time, smear over the tempered plain chocolate with the cranked palette knife so that it runs completely over all the edges of the acetate. The chocolate will soon start to set, so pick up the first piece and wrap it around a mini cake with the chocolate side against the cake, allowing one end to very slightly overlap the other (see Decorating Techniques: Working with Chocolate). Repeat with the other pieces of chocolate-covered acetate, then with the remaining pieces of acetate until you have wrapped all the cakes.

Three Place the cakes in the fridge for a few minutes to help them set, then take them out and carefully remove the acetate. You may have to pull and wiggle the acetate very gently at the end where it overlaps.

Four To finish, place a large red sugar rose, as used in the main cake, in the centre of each mini cake.

Sweetheart cookies

Hearts are a must-have for Valentine's, and these cookies really hit the spot with their deep red icing punched out by a border of pink dots.

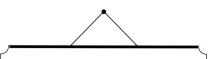

YOU'LL ALSO NEED
6.5cm (2½in) wide chocolate heart-shaped cookies, flooded with red icing (see Baking and Covering Techniques: Baking Cookies and Decorating Techniques: Royal-Iced Cookies)

Fuchsia pink-coloured soft-peak royal icing (see Decorating Techniques: Royal Icing)

No. 1.5 piping tube (tip)

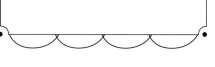

Fill a small paper piping (pastry) bag fitted with a no. 1.5 piping tube with fuchsia pink-coloured soft-peak royal icing. Pipe a border of spaced small dots around the outlined edge of the flooded area on each of the cookies (see Decorating Techniques: Piping with Royal Icing).

Dainties of desire

These gorgeous morsels of cake offer another variation on the pink/red and brown colour scheme, this time using brown-coloured flower paste decorations rather than chocolate.

One Thinly roll out some brown flower paste and use the heart cutter to cut out a heart for each fondant fancy. Stick onto the centre of each cake with a small amount of edible glue.

Two Fill a small paper piping (pastry) bag fitted with a no. 1.5 piping tube with the brown royal icing. Pipe spaced small dots around the heart edges (see Decorating Techniques: Piping with Royal Icing).

YOU'LL ALSO NEED

Fondant fancies (chocolate sponge, or vanilla sponge filled with raspberry jam), dipped in ruby-fuchsia fondant and set in brown foil cases (liners) (see Baking and Covering Techniques: Fondant Fancies)

Brown flower (petal/gum) paste

Brown-coloured soft-peak royal icing (see Decorating Techniques: Royal Icing)

3cm (1¼in) heart cutter

No. 1.5 piping tube (tip)

Edible glue

Festival
OF WHITE

Set the festive scene in cool, cutting-edge style with this shimmering pure-white scheme based on a single, bauble motif.

Whitework wonder

This sophisticated cake features delicate white-on-white piped patterns inspired by transparent baubles and a cut-out bauble edging to create an effect reminiscent of fine whitework embroidered linen. The gaps between the tiers allow the border to hang down below them and enhance the draped look.

Materials

One 10cm (4in) square and one 20cm (8in) square cake, 7.5cm (3in) deep, prepared and iced in white sugarpaste (rolled fondant) at least 12-24 hours in advance (see Recipes and Techniques)

One 15cm (6in) square and one 25cm (10in) square cake, 11.5cm (4½in) deep, prepared and iced in white sugarpaste at least 12-24 hours in advance (see Recipes and Techniques)

One 33cm (13in) square cake board, covered in white sugarpaste (see Baking and Covering Techniques: Icing Cake Boards and Dummies)

100g (3½oz) white flower (gum/petal) paste

¼ quantity white royal icing (see Decorating Techniques: Royal Icing)

FINISHES Crystal White Magic Sparkles, non-toxic white diamond glitter or pearl sprinkling sugar, pearl white edible lustre

Edible glue

Equipment

12 hollow pieces of dowel, cut to size (see Baking and Covering Techniques: Assembling Tiered Cakes)

Two 13cm (5in) square cake boards, stuck together with royal icing, and two 23cm (9in) square cake boards, stuck together with royal icing

RIBBON 1.5cm (⅝in), 1cm (⅜in), 2.5cm (1in) white satin

Needle scriber or pointed tool

CIRCLE CUTTERS 3cm (1⅛in), 3.5cm (1⅜in)

Small paper piping (pastry) bags (see Decorating Techniques: Making a Piping Bag)

No. 1 piping tube (tip)

Basic equipment (see Tools and Equipment)

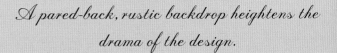

A pared-back, rustic backdrop heightens the drama of the design.

To assemble the cakes, dowel the 15cm (6in), 20cm (8in) and 25cm (10in) cakes using four dowels in each (see Baking and Covering Techniques: Assembling Tiered Cakes). Secure the 1.5cm (⅝in) ribbon around the 13cm (5in) and 23cm (9in) cake boards (see Baking and Covering Techniques: Securing Ribbon Around Cakes and Boards).

(a) Stick the 23cm (9in) cake boards in the centre of the 33cm (13in) iced cake board with royal icing. Assemble the 25cm (10in) cake, then the 20cm (8in) cake on top. Stick the 13cm (5in) cake boards on top of the 20cm (8in) tier, then stack the 15cm (6in) and 10cm (4in) tiers to complete the cake. Secure the 1cm (⅜in) ribbon around the base of each tier (see Baking and Covering Techniques: Securing Ribbon Around Cakes and Boards).

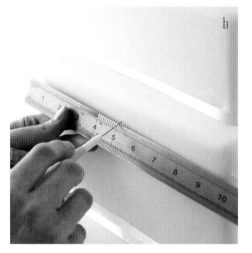

(b) *To pipe the design around the bottom tier,* using a ruler and a needle scriber or pointed tool, mark a point at each corner and then seven points an equal distance apart along each side of the tier in between and in addition to the corner points, starting about 1cm (⅜in) from the top of the cake. To do this, mark the corner and the centre point, then halfway between those marks and halfway again between the previously marked points.

Fit a small paper piping bag with the no.1 piping tube and fill with the royal icing. Starting at the left-hand side of one of the tier sides, pipe a swag of icing between each marked point, working all the way around the tier, turning the cake as you go (see Decorating Techniques: Piping with Royal Icing).

(c) Pipe a second row of swags underneath the first, but this time using the centre point of each previously piped swag as the point to start and finish the second row of swags. Finally, pipe small dots of icing over all the original marked points around the tier.

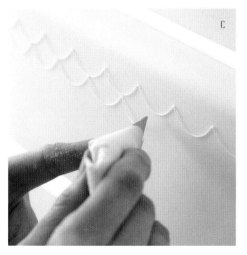

If your lines of icing break, simply scrape them off lightly and pipe them again.

Repeat the piping process for the 15cm (6in) tier, but this time use a ruler to mark four points an equal distance across each side of the tier and one on each corner. Then pipe two rows of swags as before.

For the 20cm (8in) tier, mark points in the same way as for the bottom tier, but starting 1.5–2cm (⅝–¾in) from the top of the cake. Pipe two rows of swags as before, then add a third row that alternates with the second row and matches the first. Pipe a small dot at each point. For the top tier, mark a point at the corners and in the centre of each side. Next mark points in between those already made so that all the marked points are an equal distance apart. Pipe three rows of swags and small dots as for the 20cm (8in) tier.

For the bauble decoration, thinly roll out the flower paste and use the cutters to cut out circles in the two sizes. You'll need about 52 in total.

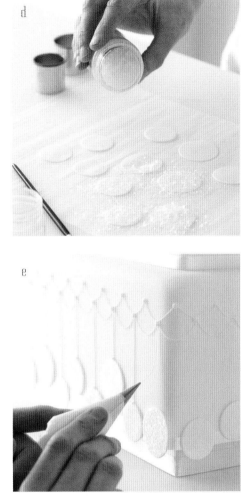

(d) Brush edible glue over one-third of the circles and sprinkle with the Magic Sparkles – you may need to do this in two or three stages as the glue dries quickly. Set aside to dry for about 20 minutes. Moisten another third of the circles with glue and sprinkle on the white diamond glitter or pearl sprinkling sugar, then set aside to dry. If using glitter, you will need to remove the bauble decoration before serving. Dust the remaining circles with pearl white lustre. Fill a new paper piping bag with royal icing. Using only a small amount, stick the discs in a random order around the bottom of the 15cm (6in) and 25cm (10in) cakes, positioning them at different heights but with the centre of each bauble directly below a point on the lower swag above.

(e) Using a fresh bag of royal icing, pipe lines from the swags down to the centre of each bauble. Pipe small dots where the lines meet the baubles and at the top where they meet the swags.

Finish by securing the 2.5cm (1in) ribbon around the base board.

When piping the vertical lines downwards, tilt the cake slightly using a book or stacked chopping boards.

Bauble beauties

My talented friend and fellow cake decorator Makiko Searle's renowned signature 'temari' ball-shaped cakes provided the inspiration for these luxurious-looking bauble cakes. The satiny pearlized finish is easily achieved by spraying the iced cakes with pearl lustre spray.

YOU'LL ALSO NEED

Ball cakes, flavour of choice, baked in about 3cm (1¼in) half-sphere moulds following the instructions for Baking Cupcakes (see Baking and Covering Techniques)

Buttercream or ganache, flavour of choice (see Fillings and Coverings)

White sugarpaste (rolled fondant)

Pearl lustre spray

Silver dragées (sugar balls)

One Level the tops of the baked cakes so that they are flat, then sandwich them together with buttercream or ganache. Coat with more buttercream or ganache and chill in the fridge for at least 20 minutes.

Two Place a ball cake on a square of baking (parchment) paper. Cover it in white sugarpaste as you would a round mini cake (see Baking and Covering Techniques: Mini Cakes), cupping and shaping the icing around the base of the cake where the ball tapers inwards. Trim the excess icing away with a small, sharp knife. Use your hands to smooth the icing instead of an icing smoother. Repeat to cover the remaining ball cakes. Leave the icing to harden for a few hours or overnight.

Three Spray with pearl lustre spray and set aside to dry for 10 minutes or so.

Four Fill a small paper piping (pastry) bag fitted with the no. 1 piping tube (tip) with white royal icing. Pipe lines of different lengths from the centre top of each bauble down the side. Pipe small dots at the end of each line. Carefully place a silver dragée at the centre top where the lines meet.

Mini crystal cream cupcakes

Buttercream-piped mini cupcakes are scattered with glitter flakes for a simple, sparkling result. Add a spoonful of mincemeat, or to taste, to the sponge mixture for extra festive flavour.

YOU'LL ALSO NEED

Mini cupcakes, flavour of choice, baked in silver foil mini cupcake cases (liners) (see Baking and Covering Techniques: Baking Cupcakes)

Buttercream, flavour of choice (see Fillings and Coverings)

Medium-large disposable plastic piping (pastry) bag

1cm (⅜in) open star piping tube (tip)

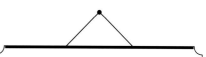 *One* Fit the piping bag with the star piping tube and fill with buttercream. Pipe a buttercream kiss onto each cupcake (see Baking and Covering Techniques: Preparing and Icing Cupcakes).

 *Two* Sprinkle Crystal White Magic Sparkles, as used in the main cake, over the freshly piped buttercream kisses.

Dazzling drops

Christmas cookies don't come more elegant than these bauble-fashioned ones, with their crisp white icing and subtle relief patterning of pretty piped tendrils.

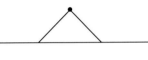

YOU'LL ALSO NEED
Bauble-shaped cookies, iced with white royal icing (see Decorating Techniques: Royal-Iced Cookies)

Very small circle cutter (optional)

One If you want to hang the cookies, cut a hole in the top of each with a very small circle cutter as soon as they come out of the oven before cooling and flooding them with royal icing.

Two Fill a small paper piping (pastry) bag fitted with the no. 1 piping tube (tip) with white royal icing. Pipe two or three curved lines onto the iced cookies, adding teardrop shapes on either side, to resemble a tendril with leaves. Fill in the teardrop shapes with a pattern of zigzag lines.

Three If you have made holes in the cookies, thread a length of 1cm (⅜in) white satin ribbon, as used in the main cake, through each hole to hang from the tree.

Christmas cake chocolate truffles

Festive traditional fruit cake crumbs mixed with ganache make a luxurious, deliciously rich filling for dark chocolate truffles, which are everybody's favourite sweetmeat. Scattered with white sprinkles, they look like they've been dusted with snowflakes.

YOU'LL ALSO NEED
Traditional fruit cake (see Recipes)

Ganache, flavour of choice
(see Fillings and Coverings)

Tempered plain (semisweet or bittersweet) chocolate (see Decorating Techniques: Working with Chocolate)

Disposable gloves

White hundreds and thousands
(nonpareils)

One Crumble the fruit cake into a mixing bowl and add a small amount of ganache to make the mixture come together (see Baking and Covering Techniques: Cake Pops). Roll the mixture into small balls and chill in the fridge briefly to firm up, also as instructed in the Cake Pops section.

Two Put on a pair of disposable gloves. Dip the cake balls one at a time into the tempered chocolate and then roll them in your hands, removing some of the excess chocolate and creating a ruffled, textured surface.

Three Carefully place the coated cake balls onto a sheet of baking (parchment) paper and immediately sprinkle them with the white hundreds and thousands before they set. Allow the chocolate to set.

To add extra Christmassy sparkle to these chocolate treats, sprinkle them with white glitter flakes.

Crispy, crunchy snowballs

These snowball-like morsels of meringue contain toasted flaked almonds for added texture and flavour. Pile them high in a glass dish hung with glistening glass beading.

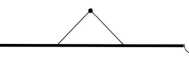

YOU'LL ALSO NEED

Meringue mix (see Baking and Covering Techniques: Meringues)

100g (3½oz) toasted flaked almonds

Baking trays (sheets) lined with silicone sheets

One Fold the toasted flaked almonds into the meringue mix.

Two Spoon dessertspoonfuls of the mixture onto the lined baking trays (sheets), spaced well apart, and bake according to the instructions given in the section on Meringues (see Baking and Covering Techniques).

Precious
pearly pops

Dipped in delicious white chocolate and encased in a gleaming pearlized coating with a glittery finish, these classy cake pops taste as good as they look.

YOU'LL ALSO NEED
Cake pops, dipped in white chocolate
(see Baking and Covering Techniques:
Cake Pops)

Pearl lustre spray

Glitter flakes sprinkles or sparkling
sugar

One Wrap some cling film (plastic wrap) around each cake pop stick to mask it and then spray the cake pops with pearl lustre.

Two Immediately sprinkle over the glitter flakes sprinkles or sparkling sugar, then leave to dry. Remove the cling film (plastic wrap) from the sticks before serving.

Lullaby
OF SWEET LOVES

Create an adorable table of tempting treats to celebrate a new baby
using pretty pastels, playful polka dots and satiny ribbon.

Washday garlands

This endearing cake design featuring washing lines of baby clothes strung around the tiers is one of my most popular choices for christenings and naming days. Instead of the usual sugarpaste, I have cut the clothing from edible printed paper, designed by Stephanie Dyment, to look like patterned fabric.

Materials

One 13cm (5in) round cake, 11.5cm (4½in) deep, and one 20cm (8in) round cake, 13cm (5in) deep, prepared and iced in pale ivory sugarpaste (rolled fondant) at least 12-24 hours in advance (see Recipes and Techniques)

One 28cm (11in) round cake board, covered in pale green sugarpaste (see Baking and Covering Techniques: Icing Cake Boards and Dummies)

100g (3½oz) chocolate-flavoured sugarpaste and ½ tsp CMC

75g (2¾oz) white flower (petal/gum) paste

35g (1¼oz) white sugarpaste

White vegetable fat (shortening)

Printed edible paper (available from sugarcraft stores/suppliers)

¼ quantity white royal icing

Ivory food colouring

Edible glue

Equipment

3 hollow pieces of dowel, cut to size (see Baking and Covering Techniques: Assembling Tiered Cakes)

RIBBON 1.5cm (⅝in) beige with cream spots grosgrain, green satin

Measuring tape

Needle scriber or pointed tool

Sugar gun

Edible pen

Small, sharp scissors

Small paper piping (pastry) bag (see Decorating Techniques: Making a Pastry Bag)

No. 1 piping tube (tip)

Basic equipment (see Tools and Equipment)

The combination of subdued colours and polka dots is perfect for the baby theme.

Macarons

To assemble the cake, dowel the two cake tiers and then set them up on the iced cake board (see Baking and Covering Techniques: Assembling Tiered Cakes).

Secure the spotted grosgrain ribbon around the base of both tiers (see Baking and Covering Techniques: Securing Ribbon Around Cakes and Boards).

Using a measuring tape and a needle scriber or pointed tool, mark four points on the base of the top tier an equal distance apart and around the top edge of the cake. Repeat for the bottom tier but marking five points instead of four.

[a] To make the washing-line poles, knead the CMC into the chocolate sugarpaste so that it becomes a little firmer. Roll about 8–9g (¼oz) into a long, thin sausage shape, first using your hands and then with an icing smoother to help create an even shape. The sausage should be 2–3mm (about ⅛in) thick and at least 30cm (12in) long (enough for two washing-line poles). Cut the sausage in half and set the pieces aside while you make seven more pieces for the two tiers.

[b] Trim the sausages neatly at one end and then stick them onto the cake at each point with a small amount of edible glue. Trim the poles at the top of the cake with a small, sharp knife.

For the washing lines, knead 25g (1oz) white flower paste into 35g (1¼oz) white sugarpaste and 3–4 teaspoons white vegetable fat. Push the paste into the sugar gun fitted with a 1mm (¹⁄₃₂in) hole attachment. Dab a small amount of edible glue on the cake just above one of the poles and above the pole to the right (if you are right-handed), and then another small amount on the cake in a curve in between the poles where the washing-line string will go.

[c] Start squeezing out the paste and allow it to hang over the first pole for support. Continue squeezing and guide the icing across to the pole on the right, allowing it to drop down slightly in between both of them. When you get to the other side, let the icing hang over the pole for support and break away the excess by pinching it. Neatly trim away the excess icing with a small, sharp knife. Repeat this process around both cakes to complete the washing lines.

For the baby clothes, transfer the clothes templates to paper and cut out, then lay them on the sheets of printed edible paper and draw around them with an edible pen. Cut them out with small, sharp scissors. You will need a mixture of different shapes of clothes and patterns, and a total of 12 items of clothing for the top tier and 15 for the bottom. Keep the sheets of printed edible paper and any cut pieces (still on their backing paper) in a plastic sleeve until you are ready to use them.

You can design your own patterns and print them out on an edible printer or email them to a sugarcraft supplier to print them for you. Otherwise, use cut-out pieces of coloured flower (petal/gum) paste.

Roll out about 25g (1oz) of white flower paste to 1mm (1/32in) thick. Choose your first item of clothing and cut a piece of flower paste slightly smaller than the edible paper shape. It doesn't have to be exactly the same shape, as it is just used to support the paper shape underneath so that it stands slightly proud of the surface of the cake.

(d) Stick the flower paste shape to the cake underneath the washing line where you will be hanging the clothes with edible glue. Peel the edible paper from its backing sheet and, using the tiniest amount of edible glue, stick it onto the flower paste shape, making sure that the top of clothing is touching the washing line.

Repeat this process until all the items of clothing are hanging on the washing lines around the two tiers.

For the pegs, colour about 2 teaspoons of royal icing with ivory food colouring until you have a light brown/caramel colour (see Decorating Techniques: Colouring Icings). Fit a small paper piping bag fitted with a no. 1 piping tube with the icing and pipe two short lines at the top of each item of clothing as if securing the clothes to the washing lines (see Decorating Techniques: Piping with Royal Icing).

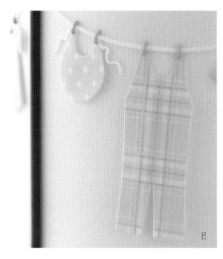

(e) *For the bib ties,* fill another paper piping bag fitted with the no. 1 tube with some white royal icing and pipe a little squiggle either side of the top of each bib.

Roll nine tiny balls from the firm brown sugarpaste and stick one to the top of each pole with edible glue.

Finish by securing the green ribbon around the base board (see Baking and Covering Techniques: Securing Ribbon Around Cakes and Boards).

Stick on the middle pieces of clothing between each pole first, then the two ones on either side so that they are evenly placed.

Meringues

Vanilla cupcake kisses

Decorate vanilla cupcakes with a whopping kiss of buttercream, then tie them into the theme with a pastel printed (non-edible) topper.

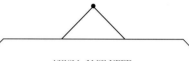

YOU'LL ALSO NEED
Vanilla cupcakes, baked in green foil cupcake cases (liners) (see Baking and Covering Techniques: Baking Cupcakes)

Vanilla-flavoured buttercream (see Fillings and Coverings)

Large disposable plastic piping (pastry) bag with large plain piping tube (tip)

Digital patterns, thin white card for printing and plain pastel card or ready-printed and plain pastel card

CRAFT PUNCHES 7.5cm (3in) scallop circle, 5cm (2in) plain circle

Cocktail sticks (toothpicks), glue and tape

One Fill the piping bag fitted with the piping tube with the vanilla buttercream and pipe a large kiss onto each cupcake.

Two Print out your own patterns from a computer onto thin card, or use ready-printed card. Use the scallop circle punch to cut pastel card circles and the plain circle punch to cut printed card circles. Glue the latter inside the former. Tape a cocktail stick to the back of each scallop circle. Insert a topper into each cake.

Polka dot parcels

These dainty little cakes are perfect for packing into individual Perspex boxes and tying with baby pink spotted ribbon in a bow as a party gift.

YOU'LL ALSO NEED
5cm (2in) square mini cakes, flavour of choice, prepared and iced in pale blue and pale green sugarpaste (rolled fondant) (see Covering and Baking Techniques: Mini Cakes)

CUTTERS Straight Garrett frill, 5mm (¼in) circle

One For the scalloped base border, thinly roll out some white flower (petal/gum) paste into a narrow strip 23–25cm (9–10in) in length. Use the Garrett frill cutter to cut a scalloped edge along the length of the icing. Cut a straight edge closely down the inside of the scallops with a sharp knife. Wrap the scalloped strip around the base of the cake and secure in place with a small amount of edible glue. Repeat for the other cakes.

Two For the polka dots, thinly roll out some more flower paste and use the circle cutter to cut out small circles. Stick them to the cakes with edible glue in a uniform pattern.

Pastel patchwork cookies

These novelty cookies extend the fabric concept of the main cake with squares of printed edible paper and a piped zigzag border to resemble stitching.

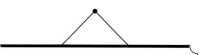

YOU'LL ALSO NEED
6cm (2½in) square vanilla-flavoured cookies, covered with sugarpaste (rolled fondant) or iced with royal icing in colours to match the edible printed paper (see Decorating Techniques: Covering Cookies with Sugarpaste or Royal-Iced Cookies)

Caramel-coloured royal icing
(see Decorating Techniques: Royal Icing)

One Cut squares of the printed edible paper used in the main cake to match the size of the icing area on the cookies. Peel them from the backing paper and stick to the cookies with a small amount of edible glue.

Two Fill a small paper piping (pastry) bag fitted with the no. 1 tube (tip) with caramel-coloured royal icing and pipe a zigzag border around the edges of the squares.

Lemony lollipop cake pops

These yellow-coated and sugared cake pops are a bright, playful addition to the table. Tied up in cellophane, they are also fun for kids to unwrap.

YOU'LL ALSO NEED
Uncoated cake pops, chilled
(see Baking and Covering Techniques:
Cake Pops)

Yellow Candy Melts

Lemon sprinkling sugar

Cellophane and white satin ribbon

One Melt the Candy Melts as instructed in the section on Cake Pops (see Baking and Covering Techniques). Dip the cake pops into the melted candy one at a time, then transfer to a sheet of baking (parchment) paper and immediately sprinkle with the lemon sugar.

Two Leave the cake pops to dry, then wrap each in a 20cm (8in) square of cellophane and tie with the ribbon in a bow.

Cake Pops

Baby blue meringue moments

These gorgeously cute sweet mouthfuls match the scheme perfectly with their pale blue colour. They also offer a little extra treat – a white chocolate bottom!

YOU'LL ALSO NEED

Meringue mix, coloured with baby blue food colouring (see Baking and Covering Techniques: Meringues)

Large disposable plastic piping (pastry) bag

8mm (³⁄₈in) plain tube (tip)

Baking trays (sheets) lined with silicone sheets

Tempered white chocolate (see Decorating Techniques: Working with Chocolate)

One Fill the plastic piping bag fitted with the piping tube with some of the meringue and pipe kisses onto the lined baking trays (sheets), spaced well apart. Bake according to the instructions given in the section on Meringues (see Baking and Covering Techniques).

Two Once the meringues have cooled, dip the bases of the meringues one at a time into the tempered white chocolate and place them on a sheet of baking (parchment) paper to set.

Minty green
macaroon crackers

Pretty pastel macaroons are packaged up as identical twins in cellophane to make charming see-through crackers, tied at each end with complementary ribbon.

One Place two macaroons together side by side and wrap a square of cellophane around them.

Two Tie a length of the satin ribbon around either end, finishing in a bow.

YOU'LL ALSO NEED
Pale bluey-green macaroons, filled with blue-green-coloured buttercream or white ganache, flavour of choice (see Baking and Covering Techniques: Macaroons)

20cm (8in) cellophane squares and beige satin ribbon

At the
CAKE PARLOUR

This classy collection of cakes and confectionery has been created around our unique Cake Parlour branding.

Silhouette and stripe statement

The centrepiece cake features our signature striped backdrop and lady silhouette motif, on the deepest tier for maximum impact. The silhouette is simple to create using a laser-cut stencil (from Designer Stencils – see the Suppliers section). Have fun devising your own motif, or look online for sources of silhouette images.

Materials

One 25cm (10in) and one 13cm (5in) round cake, 9cm (3½in) deep, prepared and iced in white sugarpaste (rolled fondant) at least 12-24 hours in advance (see Recipes and Techniques)

One 18cm (7in) round cake, 14cm (5½in) deep, prepared and iced in pale willow green (Wilton)-coloured sugarpaste at least 12-24 hours in advance (see Recipes and Techniques)

One 30cm (12in) round cake board, covered with black sugarpaste (see Baking and Covering Techniques: Icing Cake Boards and Dummies)

150g (5½oz) white flower (petal/gum) paste

½ quantity royal icing (see Decorating Techniques: Royal Icing)

FOOD COLOURING claret (Sugarflair), willow green (Wilton), black

Edible glue

Equipment

7 hollow pieces of dowels, cut to size (see Baking and Covering Techniques: Assembling Tiered Cakes)

CUTTERS 8cm (3¼in) fluted/plain oval (PME), 7mm (5⁄16in) circle

RIBBON 7mm (5⁄16in) black grosgrain, 1.5cm (5⁄8in) black satin

Custom-made laser-cut silhouette stencil, about 5.5-6cm (2¼-2³⁄8in) high

Basic equipment (see Tools and Equipment)

For the cake and filling flavouring, vanilla, lemon or chocolate are ideal, popular choices.

Start by dowelling and assembling the cake on the cake board (see Baking and Covering Techniques: Assembling Tiered Cakes). You will need four dowels in the bottom tier and three in the middle tier.

To make the oval plaque for the silhouette, first colour 75g (2¾oz) of the white flower paste with claret food colouring to make a medium pink colour (see Decorating Techniques: Colouring Icings). Roll out about 20g (¾oz) of the paste until it is about 2mm (¹/₁₆in) thick and use the fluted side of the oval cutter to cut out an oval shape. Once cut, gently roll over the shape to make it slightly larger all round.

(a) Roll out about 10g (¼oz) of the white flower paste about 1mm (¹/₃₂in) thick and use the plain side of the oval cutter to cut out an oval. Stick the white oval onto the pink fluted oval with a small amount of edible glue. Set aside for a few hours to dry.

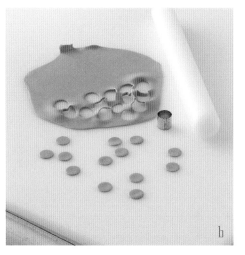

> *Create two or three oval plaques*
> *in case you make any mistakes*
> *when you are stencilling on your*
> *silhouette with black icing.*

To decorate the base of the top and bottom tiers, wrap the 7mm (⁵/₁₆in) black grosgrain ribbon around each of the tiers and secure in place with double-sided tape (see Baking and Covering Techniques: Securing Ribbon Around Cakes and Boards).

(b) Roll out the remaining pink flower paste thinly and use the circle cutter to cut out 50–60 circles – you will need about 20 for the top tier and 30 or more for the bottom tier.

(c) Cut each pink circle in half to form semicircles. Using edible glue, stick the semicircles around both tiers, placing them side by side to form a scallop border above the ribbon.

Colour the remaining 65g (2½oz) of the white flower paste with the willow green food colouring to make a medium green and thinly roll out about 30g (1oz) so that its length is slightly longer than the depth of the middle tier of the cake. Using a large, sharp knife, cut thin strips of paste about 1cm (³⁄₈in) wide. You will need about 24 strips to go around the tier, so simply roll out more of the green-coloured paste until you have enough.

(d) and (e) Using edible glue, stick the green strips around the middle tier about 1.3cm (½in) apart. Line up the bottom of the strip against the base of the tier and trim the strip at the top where it meets the top tier with a small, sharp knife.

(f) Colour about 2 tablespoons of the royal icing black, and make sure that the consistency is soft peak (see Decorating Techniques: Royal Icing).

(g) Position the stencil centrally on the white centre of plaque and thinly smear over some of the black royal icing, taking care not to move the stencil while doing so. Carefully lift off the stencil to reveal the silhouette. Leave to dry.

Once the silhouette has dried, stick the plaque in the centre of the side of the middle tier with some royal icing. You may have to hold the plaque in place for a moment until it is well adhered.

Finish by securing the 1.5cm (⁵⁄₈in) black satin ribbon around the base board with double-sided tape (see Baking and Covering Techniques: Securing Ribbon Around Cakes and Boards).

Pretty portrait cookies

These cookies echo the design of the main cake wonderfully. You could also bake them on sticks to display them upright in glasses filled with coloured sugar.

One Roll out the medium pink sugarpaste until about 3mm (⅛in) thick and use the fluted side of the oval cutter to cut out an oval shape for each cookie. Stick them onto the cookies with a small amount of the apricot masking spread or strained jam (see Decorating Techniques: Covering Cookies with Sugarpaste).

Two Roll out the white sugarpaste until 2–3mm (¹⁄₁₆–⅛in) thick and use the plain side of the oval cutter to cut out an equal number of plain ovals. Stick them onto the cookies inside the pink scalloped border. Leave to dry for an hour or two before stencilling on the black silhouette as described for the main cake. Leave to dry again.

YOU'LL ALSO NEED
Fluted oval-shaped vanilla-flavoured cookies, cut out with the oval cutter used in the main cake (see Baking and Covering Techniques: Baking Cookies)

Sugarpaste (rolled fondant): medium pink, white

Boiled, cooled apricot masking spread or strained jam

Cameo cupcakes

Make the plaque featured in the main cake as miniature cameos and use to decorate cupcakes topped with swirls of buttercream. The cupcakes look really stunning in black cases presented on a black cake stand to match.

YOU'LL ALSO NEED

Cupcakes, flavour of choice, baked in black cupcake cases (liners) (see Baking and Covering Techniques: Baking Cupcakes)

Buttercream, flavour to match or complement cupcakes (see Fillings and Coverings)

4.5cm (1¾in) fluted/plain oval cutter (PME)

Custom-made laser-cut silhouette stencil, about 3cm (1¼in) high

Large disposable plastic piping (pastry) bag

Large star tube (tip)

One 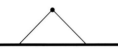 Make plaques as for the main cake but using the smaller oval cutter. Leave to dry completely flat.

Two Fill the piping bag fitted with the large star tube with buttercream and pipe large swirls onto the cupcakes (see Baking and Covering Techniques: Preparing and Icing cupcakes). Push the cameos into the buttercream, positioning them to stand fairly upright.

Candy-stripe
and bowtie minis

These mix-and-match mini cakes make an elegant display. One design uses the stripe and scallop combination of the main cake, while the other features stylish pale pink stripes that create a pin-tuck effect, topped off with a black bowtie. These sugar bows are simple to make and can be prepared in advance to ease the pressure on the day.

YOU'LL ALSO NEED

5cm (2in) round mini cakes, some prepared and iced in pale willow green (Wilton)-coloured and the remainder in white sugarpaste (rolled fondant) about 3 hours in advance (see Baking and Covering Techniques: Mini Cakes)

5cm (2in) circle cutter

1 quantity soft-peak royal icing (see Decorating Techniques: Royal Icing)

Small paper piping (pastry) bags (see Decorating Techniques: Making a Piping Bag)

No. 1.5 piping tube (tip)

One For the candy-stripe design, use the circle cutter to gently mark a circle around the top edge of each cake. Thinly roll out some medium green flower (petal/gum) paste, as used in the main cake, and cut strips about 1cm (3⁄8in) wide and slightly longer than the depth of the mini cakes. You will need eight strips of paste per cake. Stick the strips around the sides of the cakes about 1.3cm (1⁄2in) apart with a small amount of edible glue. Trim the strips on the top of the cake to end at the circular indentation.

Two Colour a little of the royal icing medium pink with the claret food colouring used for the main cake (see Decorating Techniques: Colouring Icings), fill a piping bag fitted with a no. 1.5 piping tube and pipe three evenly spaced dots along the top edge of each green strip (see Decorating Techniques: Piping with Royal Icing). Stick medium pink flower paste semicircles, as used in the main cake, side by side down the left-hand edge of each strip.

Three To make the bowtie cakes, for the bows, cut out 1.5cm (5⁄8in) wide strips 15cm (6in) long from thinly rolled-out black flower paste. Form each strip into bow loops by turning in either end to meet and pinching in the centre. For the knots, wrap a strip 5mm (1⁄4in) wide and 2cm (3⁄4in) long around the centre of each set of loops and join at the back with edible glue.

Four Colour the remaining royal icing pale pink with claret food colouring and fill a piping bag fitted with a no. 1.5 piping tube. Pipe strips about 3mm (1⁄8in) apart around each cake, starting from the centre of the cake running down to the base. Squeeze out a small ball of icing at the bottom of each stripe. Leave to dry.

Five When the stripes are dry, stick a sugar bow to the top of each cake with edible glue, or royal icing if the bow is completely dry.

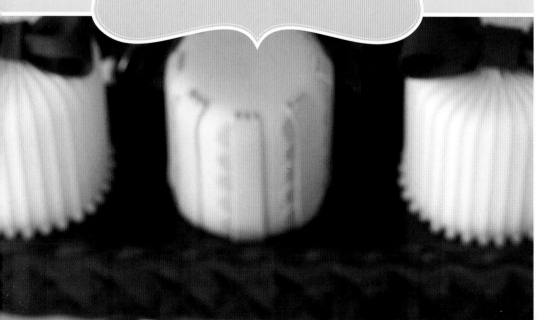

These dreamily light meringues look so much the part here in pastel pink. They make the perfect decadent addition to our Cake Parlour sweet table.

Powder pink parlour puffs

YOU'LL ALSO NEED
Meringue mix (see Baking and
Covering Techniques: Meringues)

Baking trays (sheets) lined with
silicone sheets

One Add the claret food colouring used in the main cake to the meringue mix until you have a pale pink colour (see Baking and Covering Techniques: Meringues).

Two Spoon dessertspoonful-size mounds of the mix onto the lined baking trays, spaced well apart, and bake according to the instructions in the section on Meringues (see Baking and Covering Techniques).

Chic striped squares

YOU'LL ALSO NEED
Fondant fancies, dipped in medium
willow green (Wilton)-coloured fondant,
set in black paper cases (liners) (see
Baking and Covering Techniques:
Fondant Fancies)

The striped scheme of The Cake Parlour is applied to these fancies with a fresh twist by attaching a wide band of white flower paste to the centre of the cake top. The same pink scallop border featured in the main cake adds an extra touch of refinement, and black paper cases complete the coordinating look.

One Cut strips of thinly rolled-out white flower (petal/gum) paste about 2cm (¾in) wide and 6cm (2½in) long, one for each cake. Lay a strip down the centre of each cake, tucking the ends into the case.

Two Using edible glue, stick medium pink flower paste semicircles, as used in the main cake, side by side down either side of each white strip.

Perfectly pink
macaroons

Crisp, colourful macaroons are one of our favourite speciality confections at The Cake Parlour. Dust the tops lightly with edible lustre dust when cooled for an inviting gleam and pile them up on a black cake stand for extra drama.

YOU'LL ALSO NEED
Macaroon mix (see Baking and Covering Techniques: Macaroons)

Filling of choice (see Fillings and Coverings)

Baking trays (sheets) lined with silicone sheets

Pink edible shimmer/lustre dust

One Add claret food colouring, as used for the main cake, to the macaroon mix to make it a medium pink colour, then prepare and bake the macaroon shells following the instructions in Macaroons (see Baking and Covering Techniques).

Two Once the macaroon shells are cool, sandwich them together with your chosen filling. Lightly dust pink edible shimmer/lustre dust over the macaroons to make them shine.

Tools and Equipment

The following is a checklist of essential equipment plus the tools you'll need for your creative work, as well as items for assembly, presentation and display, most of which are non-reusable. Any specific tools that are required in addition to the basics are itemized in the individual projects.

Basic equipment

Large electric mixer for making cakes, cookies, meringues, macaroons, buttercream and royal icing

Kitchen scales and measuring spoons for weighing out ingredients

Mixing bowls for mixing ingredients

Sieve (strainer) for sifting dry ingredients

Spatulas for mixing and gently folding cake mixtures together

Cake tins (pans) for baking cakes

Tartlet tins (pans) and/or muffin trays (pans) for baking cupcakes

Baking trays (sheets) for baking cookies

Metal skewer to test cakes for doneness

Plastic trays for putting baked cookies, cupcakes and decorations on

Wire racks for cooling cakes and icing fondant fancies

Greaseproof (wax) paper or baking (parchment) paper and scissors for lining tins, and for placing under icing during preparation

Cling film (plastic wrap) to cover icing to stop drying out and to wrap cookie dough

Large non-stick board to put icing and marzipan on when rolling it out

Non-slip mat to put under the board so that it doesn't slip on the work surface

Large and small non-stick rolling pins for rolling out icing and marzipan

Large and small sharp knife for cutting and shaping icing

Large serrated knife for cutting cakes for layering and square mini cakes, and for cutting hollow plastic dowels to length

Cake leveller for cutting even, level layers of sponge

Large and small palette knife for applying buttercream and ganache

Icing or marzipan spacers to give a guide to thickness when rolling out

Icing smoothers for smoothing icing

Spirit level to check that cakes are level when stacking them

Metal ruler for measuring

Double-sided tape to attach ribbon around cakes, boards and pillars

Cake scraper to scrape and smooth buttercream, ganache or royal icing, used in a similar way to a palette knife

Pastry brush to brush sugar syrup and masking spread or strained jam onto cakes

Creative tools

Turntable for layering cakes and piping work

Piping (pastry) bags for royal icing decorations

Piping tubes (tips) for piping royal icing

Cocktail sticks (toothpicks) or cel sticks for colouring icing

Acetate sheets for run-out icing decorations, or for covering icing if you are interrupted while working to keep it from drying out

Edible glue for sticking icing to icing

Needle scriber or marking tool for lightly scoring positioning guides and bursting bubbles in icing

Cake-top marking template for finding/marking the centre of cakes and marking where dowels should be placed

Fine paintbrushes for gluing and painting

Dusting brushes for brushing edible dust onto icing

Dipping forks for dipping fondant fancies into fondant icing

Ball tool for frilling or thinning the edge of flower (petal/gum) paste

Foam pad for softening and frilling flower paste

Frill cutters for cutting borders and pretty edges

Circle cutters for cutting circles of various sizes

Shaped cutters for cutting out shapes such as hearts, baubles and boiled sweets (hard candy)

Assembly, presentation and display items

Hollow plastic dowels for supporting multi-tiered cakes

Round and square cake boards for supporting cakes

Cake card for placing under mini cakes

Cupcake cases (liners) for baking cupcakes

Lollipop/cake pop sticks for inserting into cake pops

Perspex boxes for storing and displaying small cakes and cupcakes

Cake stands for presenting small cakes and cupcakes

Ribbons for decorating cakes and cake boards

Recipes and Techniques

Cake Recipes

You want your cakes to taste delicious as well as look fabulous, so always source the best-quality ingredients to ensure a superior flavour. You also want to achieve a professional, crust-free finish and to do this you need to bake your cake in a tin that's 2.5cm (1in) larger than the required final dimensions. The sizes and quantities specified in the charts that follow in this section will make cakes about 9cm (3½in) deep. For shallower cakes, mini cakes and fondant fancies, use smaller quantities (see Mini Cakes and Fondant Fancies).

Measuring in cups

If you prefer to use US cup measurements, please use the following conversions.

Liquid
1 tsp = 5ml
1 tbsp = 15ml (or 20ml for Australia)
½ cup = 120ml/4fl oz
1 cup = 240ml/8½fl oz

Caster (superfine) **sugar/brown sugar**
½ cup = 100g/3½oz
1 cup = 200g/7oz

Butter
1 tbsp = 15g/½oz
2 tbsp = 25g//1oz
½ cup/1 stick = 115g/4oz
1 cup/2 sticks = 225g/8oz

Icing (confectioners') **sugar**
1 cup = 115g/4oz

Flour
1 cup = 125g/4½oz

Desiccated (dry unsweetened shredded) **coconut**
1 cup = 90g/3¼oz

Sultanas (golden raisins)
165g/5¾oz

Preparing cake tins

It's important to line the bottom and sides of your cake tin (pan) properly before adding the cake mixture and baking it to prevent the cake from sticking.

One Grease the inside of the tin with a little melted butter or sunflower oil spray first to help the paper stick and sit securely in the tin without curling up.

Two For round cakes, to line the bottom, lay your tin on a piece of greaseproof (wax) paper or baking (parchment) paper and draw around it using an edible pen. Using scissors, cut on the inside of the line so that the circle will be a good fit. Put to one side. Cut a long strip of the paper at least 9cm (3½in) wide, fold over one of the long sides about 1cm (⅜in) and crease firmly, then open out. Cut slits from the edge nearest to the fold up to the fold 2.5cm (1in) apart. Put the strip around the inside of tin, with the fold tucked into the bottom corner, then add the circle and smooth down.

Three For square cakes, lay a piece of greaseproof or baking paper over the top of the tin. Cut a square that overlaps it on each side by 7.5cm (3in). Cut a slit at each end on two opposite sides. Push the paper inside the tin and fold in the flaps.

Cake portion guide

The following chart indicates about how many portions the different sizes of cake will make. The number of portions specified is based on each piece of cake being about 2.5cm (1in) square and 9cm (3½in) deep. As fruit cake is much richer, you may consider allowing for smaller portions.

size	10cm (4in)		13cm (5in)		15cm (6in)		18cm (7in)		20cm (8in)		23cm (9in)		25cm (10in)		28cm (11in)	
Shape	O	Sq	O	Sq	O	Sq	O	Sq	O	Sq	O	Sq	O	Sq	O	Sq
Portions	5	10	10	15	20	25	30	40	40	50	50	65	65	85	85	100

Classic sponge cake

For a really light sponge cake, it's better to separate the mixture between two tins. If you want three layers for your cake, split the mixture one-third/two-thirds. For smaller cakes, you can also cut three layers of sponge from a larger square cake. For example, a 15cm (6in) round cake can be cut from a 30cm (12in) square cake (see Note above chart and also Baking and Covering Techniques: Layering, Filling and Preparation).

One Preheat your oven to 160°C/325°F/Gas Mark 3 and line your tins (pans) (see Preparing Cake Tins).

Two In a large electric mixer, beat the butter and sugar together until light and fluffy. Add the eggs gradually, beating well between each addition, then add the flavouring.

Three Sift the flour, add to the mixture and mix very carefully until just combined.

Four Remove the bowl from the mixer and fold the mixture through gently with a spatula to finish. Tip the mixture into your prepared tin or tins and spread with a palette knife or the back of a spoon.

Five Bake in the oven until a skewer inserted into the centre of your cakes comes out clean. The baking time will vary depending on your oven. Check small cakes after 20 minutes and larger cakes after 40 minutes.

Six Leave to cool, then wrap the cake well in cling film (plastic wrap) and refrigerate until ready to use.

Deeper cakes

For deeper cakes, simply bake up to one and a half times the recipe. You may need to do this in two batches if you only have a couple of tins. Leave the cakes to cool slightly before turning them out and refilling the tins with the mixture.

Shelf life

Sponges should be made up to 24 hours in advance. Freeze the sponges if they are not being used the next day. After the 1–2-day process of layering and covering the cakes, the finished cakes should last up to 3–4 days out of the fridge.

NOTE If cutting three layers from a larger square cake: for a 15cm (6in) round cake, bake an 8-egg/400g (14oz) butter etc. mix in a 30cm (12in) square tin; for a 13cm (5in) round or square cake, bake a 7-egg/350g (12oz) mix in a 28cm (11in) square tin; for a 10cm (4in) round or square cake, bake a 6-egg/300g (10½oz) mix in a 25cm (10in) square tin. Add 5–10 per cent extra flour for deeper tiers or if you find that your sponges are too soft to work with.

Cake size round square	13cm (5in) 10cm (4in)	15cm (6in) 13cm (5in)	18cm (7in) 15cm (6in)	20cm (8in) 18cm (7in)	23cm (9in) 20cm (8in)	25cm (10in) 23cm (9in)	28cm (11in) 25cm (10in)	30cm (12in) 28cm (11in)
Unsalted butter	150g (5½oz)	200g (7oz)	250g (9oz)	325g (11½oz)	450g (1lb)	525g (1lb 3oz)	625g (1lb 6oz)	800g (1lb 12oz)
Caster (superfine) sugar	150g (5½oz)	200g (7oz)	250g (9oz)	325g (11½oz)	450g (1lb)	525g (1lb 3oz)	625g (1lb 6oz)	800g (1lb 12oz)
Medium eggs	3	4	5	6	9	10	12	14
Vanilla extract (tsp)	½	1	1	1½	2	2	2½	4
Self-raising (-rising) **flour**	150g (5½oz)	200g (7oz)	250g (9oz)	325g (11½oz)	450g (1lb)	525g (1lb 3oz)	625g (1lb 6oz)	800g (1lb 12oz)

Additional flavourings

LEMON Add the finely grated zest of 1 lemon per 100g (3½oz) sugar.

ORANGE Add the finely grated zest of 2 oranges per 250g (9oz) sugar.

CHOCOLATE Replace 15g (½oz) flour with 15g (½oz) cocoa powder (unsweetened cocoa) per 100g (3½oz) flour.

BANANA Replace the caster (superfine) sugar with brown sugar. Add 1 mashed overripe banana and ½ teaspoon mixed spice (apple pie spice) per 100g (3½oz) flour.

COFFEE AND WALNUT Replace 15g (½oz) flour with 15g (½oz) finely chopped walnuts per 100g (3½oz) flour. Replace the caster (superfine) sugar with brown sugar and add cooled shots of espresso coffee to taste.

Classic chocolate cake

This recipe makes a chocolate cake with a wonderfully light texture, and it's also quick and easy. Make sure you split the mixture between two tins, dividing it equally or, for a three-layered cake, into one-third and two-thirds. For a really sumptuous result, fill with ganache rather than buttercream (see Fillings and Coverings).

Any leftovers of chocolate cake can be used for making cake pops (see Cake Pops) or truffles.

One Preheat your oven to 160°C/325°F/Gas Mark 3 and line your tins (pans) (see Preparing Cake Tins).

Two Sift the flour, cocoa and baking powder together.

Three In a large electric mixer, beat the butter and sugar together until light and fluffy. Meanwhile, crack your eggs into a separate bowl.

Four Add the eggs to the mixture gradually, beating well between each addition.

Five Add half the dry ingredients and mix until just combined before adding half the milk. Repeat with the remaining ingredients. Mix until the mixture starts to come together.

Six Finish mixing the ingredients together by hand with a spatula, and spoon into your prepared tins.

Seven Bake in the oven until a skewer inserted into the centre of your cakes comes out clean. The baking time will vary depending on your oven. Check smaller cakes after 20 minutes and larger cakes after 40 minutes.

Eight Leave to cool, then wrap the cakes well in cling film (plastic wrap) and refrigerate until ready to use.

Deeper cakes

For deeper cakes, simply bake up to one and a half times the recipe. You may need to do this in two batches if you only have a couple of tins. Leave the cakes to cool slightly before turning them out and refilling the tins with the mixture.

Shelf life

Chocolate cakes should be made up to 24 hours in advance. Freeze the cakes if they are not being used the next day. After the 1–2-day process of layering and covering the cakes, the finished chocolate cakes should last up to 3–4 days out of the fridge.

Cake size								
round	13cm (5in)	15cm (6in)	18cm (7in)	20cm (8in)	23cm (9in)	25cm (10in)	28cm (11in)	30cm (12in)
square	10cm (4in)	13cm (5in)	15cm (6in)	18cm (7in)	20cm (8in)	23cm (9in)	25cm (10in)	28cm (11in)
Plain (all-purpose) flour	170g (6oz)	225g (8oz)	280g (10oz)	365g (12½oz)	500g (1lb 2oz)	585g (1lb 4½oz)	700g (1lb 9oz)	825g (1lb 13oz)
Cocoa powder (un-sweetened cocoa)	30g (1oz)	40g (1½oz)	50g (1¾oz)	65g (2¼oz)	90g (3¼oz)	100g (3½oz)	125g (4½oz)	150g (5½oz)
Baking powder (tsp)	1½	2	2½	3¼	4½	5¼	6¼	7½
Unsalted butter	150g (5½oz)	200g (7oz)	250g (9oz)	325g (11½oz)	450g (1lb)	525g (1lb 3oz)	625g (1lb 6oz)	750g (1lb 10oz)
Caster (superfine) sugar	130g (4½oz)	175g (6oz)	220g (8oz)	285g (10oz)	400g (14oz)	460g (1lb)	550g (1lb 4oz)	650g (1lb 7oz)
Large eggs	2½	3	4	5	7	8½	10	12
Full-fat (whole) milk	100ml (3½fl oz)	135ml (4½fl oz)	170ml (5¾fl oz)	220ml (7¾fl oz)	300ml (10fl oz)	350ml (12fl oz)	425ml (15fl oz)	500ml (18fl oz)

Additional flavourings

ORANGE Use the finely grated zest of 1 orange per 2 eggs.

COFFEE LIQUEUR Add 1 cooled shot of espresso coffee per 2–3 eggs and add coffee liqueur to taste to the sugar syrup (see Fillings and Coverings).

CHOCOLATE HAZELNUT Replace 10 per cent of the flour with the same quantity of ground hazelnuts and layer with chocolate hazelnut spread and ganache (see Fillings and Coverings).

Carrot cake

The addition of chopped pecans to this carrot cake mixture not only gives it an extra flavour dimension but a great texture too. I would recommend sandwiching together two layers only with a single layer of buttercream to make one tier, in which case you need to divide the cake mixture between two tins for baking. For a perfect flavour combination, choose lemon-flavoured buttercream for the filling (see Fillings and Coverings).

You can replace the pecans with walnuts, hazelnuts or a mixture of nuts, if you prefer.

One Preheat your oven to 160°C/325°F/Gas Mark 3 and line your tins (pans) (see Preparing Cake Tins).

Two In a large electric mixer, beat together the sugar and vegetable oil for about 1 minute until the ingredients are well combined.

Three Crack your eggs into a separate bowl and add them to the mixture one at a time, beating well between each addition.

Four Sift together the dry ingredients and add them to the cake mixture, alternating with the grated carrot.

Five Fold in the chopped pecans.

Six Divide the mixture between the two prepared tins and bake in the oven for 20–50 minutes, depending on size. Check that the cakes are cooked by inserting a skewer into the centre, which should come out clean.

Seven Leave to cool, then wrap the cakes well in cling film (plastic wrap) and refrigerate until ready to use.

Deeper cakes

For deeper cakes, simply bake up to one and a half times the recipe. You may need to do this in two batches if you only have a couple of tins. Leave the cakes to cool slightly before turning them out and refilling the tins with the mixture.

Shelf life

Carrot cakes should be made up to 24 hours in advance. Freeze the cakes if they are not being used the next day. After the 1–2-day process of layering and covering the cakes, the finished carrot cakes should last up to 3–4 days out of the fridge.

Cake size								
round	13cm (5in)	15cm (6in)	18cm (7in)	20cm (8in)	23cm (9in)	25cm (10in)	28cm (11in)	30cm (12in)
square	10cm (4in)	13cm (5in)	15cm (6in)	18cm (7in)	20cm (8in)	23cm (9in)	25cm (10in)	28cm (11in)
Brown sugar	135g (4½oz)	180g (6oz)	250g (9oz)	320g (11oz)	385g (13½oz)	525g (1lb 3oz)	560g (1lb 4oz)	735g (1lb 9½oz)
Vegetable oil	135ml (4½fl oz)	180ml (6fl oz)	250ml (9fl oz)	320ml (11fl oz)	385ml (13½fl oz)	525ml (18½fl oz)	560ml (19fl oz)	735ml (25fl oz)
Medium eggs	2	2½	3	4	5	6½	7	9
Self-raising (-rising) **flour**	200g (7oz)	275g (9½oz)	375g (13oz)	480g (1lb 1oz)	590g (1lb 5oz)	775g (1lb 11oz)	850g (1lb 14oz)	1.1kg (2lb 7oz)
Mixed spice (apple pie spice) **(tbsp)**	1	1½	2	2½	3	4	4½	5½
Bicarbonate of soda (baking soda) **(tsp)**	¼	½	¾	¾	1	1	1¼	1½
Finely grated carrot	300g (10½oz)	385g (13½oz)	525g (1lb 3oz)	675g (1lb 8oz)	825g (1lb 13oz)	1.05kg (2lb 5oz)	1.2kg (2lb 10½oz)	1.5kg (3lb 5oz)
Finely chopped pecans	65g (2¼oz)	85g (3oz)	120g (4¼oz)	150g (5½oz)	175g (6oz)	240g (8½oz)	270g (9½oz)	350g (12oz)

Traditional fruit cake

After many years of trying different fruit cake recipes, this one is a firm favourite. You can vary the types of dried fruit used or, for convenience, use a pack of ready-mixed dried fruit. My choice of alcohol for flavouring is a mix of equal quantities cherry and regular brandy, but you can use rum, sherry or whisky instead. Soak your dried fruit and mixed candied peel in the alcohol for at least 24 hours beforehand. For the best results, leave the baked cake to mature for at least 1 month before serving. During the storage time, you can 'feed' your cake with your chosen alcohol once every week or two to improve the flavour still further and keep it really moist. For an even coating, use a spray bottle to spray the alcohol over the surface. Leave to soak in for 1–2 minutes, then rewrap.

Deeper cakes

Unfortunately, fruit cakes can't be made any bigger than the height of the tin. If you need to give your fruit cake a little extra height, you can double-board it (place it on two cake boards stuck together with royal icing) or add a thicker layer of marzipan to the top of the cake before icing it. All fruit cakes are covered with marzipan before being iced.

Shelf life

Fruit cakes should be made at least 4–6 weeks before being served to allow enough time for them to mature. Fruit cakes can be stored for up to 9 months or frozen to preserve their shelf life further.

One Preheat your oven to 150°C/300°F/Gas Mark 2 and line your tin (pan) with two layers of greaseproof (wax) paper or baking (parchment) paper for small cakes, and three layers for larger cakes (see Preparing Cake Tins).

Two In a large electric mixer, beat the butter and sugar together with the lemon and orange zest until fairly light and fluffy. Add the orange juice to the soaked fruit and mixed candied peel.

Three Gradually add your eggs, one at a time, beating well between each addition.

Four Sift the flour and spices together and add half the flour mixture together with half the soaked fruit mixture to the cake mixture. Mix until just combined and then add the remaining flour mixture and fruit mixture.

Five Gently fold in the ground almonds and treacle with a large metal spoon until all the ingredients are combined and then spoon the mixture into your prepared baking tin.

Six Cover the top loosely with some more greaseproof or baking paper and then bake in the oven for the time indicated or until a skewer inserted into the centre comes out clean.

Seven Pour some more alcohol over the cake while it's still hot and leave to cool in the tin.

Eight Remove from the tin and wrap your cake in a layer of greaseproof paper and then foil to store.

Cake size round square	10cm (4in) 10cm (4in)	13cm (5in) 13cm (5in)	15cm (6in) 15cm (6in)	18cm (7in) 18cm (7in)	20cm (8in) 20cm (8in)	23cm (9in) 23cm (9in)	25cm (10in) 25cm (10in)	28cm (11in) 28cm (11in)	30cm (12in) 30cm (11in)
Currants	100g (3½oz)	125g (4½oz)	175g (6oz)	225g (8oz)	300g (10½oz)	375g (13oz)	450g (1lb)	550g (1lb 4oz)	660g (1lb 7½oz)
Raisins	125g (4½oz)	150g (5½oz)	200g (7oz)	275g (9½oz)	350g (12oz)	450g (1lb)	555g (1lb 4oz)	675g (1lb 8oz)	800g (1lb 12oz)
Sultanas (golden raisins)	125g (4½oz)	150g (5½oz)	200g (7oz)	275g (9½oz)	350g (12oz)	450g (1lb)	555g (1lb 4oz)	675g (1lb 8oz)	800g (1lb 12oz)
Glacé (candied) cherries	40g (1½oz)	50g (1¾oz)	70g (2½oz)	100g (3½oz)	125g (4½oz)	150g (5½oz)	180g (6oz)	200g (7oz)	250g (9oz)
Mixed candied peel	25g (1oz)	30g (1oz)	45g (1½oz)	50g (1¾oz)	70g (2½oz)	85g (3oz)	110g (4oz)	125g (4½oz)	150g (5½oz)
Cherry brandy & brandy mix (tbsp)	2	2½	3	3½	5	6	7	8	9
Slightly salted butter	100g (3½oz)	125g (4½oz)	175g (6oz)	225g (8oz)	350g (12oz)	375g (13oz)	450g (1lb)	550g (1lb 4oz)	660g (1lb 7½oz)
Brown sugar	100g (3½oz)	125g (4½oz)	175g (6oz)	225g (8oz)	350g (12oz)	375g (13oz)	450g (1lb)	550g (1lb 4oz)	660g (1lb 7½oz)
Grated zest of lemon (per fruit)	¼	½	¾	1	1½	2	2	2½	3
Grated zest of small orange (per fruit)	¼	½	¾	1	1½	2	2	2½	3
Juice of small orange (per fruit)	¼	¼	½	½	¾	¾	1	1½	1½
Medium eggs	2	2½	3	4½	6	7	8½	10	12
Plain (all- purpose) flour	100g (3½oz)	125g (4½oz)	175g (6oz)	225g (8oz)	350g (12oz)	375g (13oz)	450g (1lb)	550g (1lb 4oz)	660g (1lb 7½oz)
Mixed spice (apple pie spice) (tsp)	½	½	¾	¾	1	1¼	1½	1½	1¾
Ground nutmeg (tsp)	¼	¼	½	½	½	¾	¾	1	1
Ground almonds	10g (¼oz)	15g (½oz)	20g (¾oz)	25g (1oz)	35g (1¼oz)	45g (1½oz)	55g (2oz)	65g (2¼oz)	75g (2¾oz)
Flaked (slivered) almonds	10g (¼oz)	15g (½oz)	20g (¾oz)	25g (1oz)	35g (1¼oz)	45g (1½oz)	55g (2oz)	65g (2¼oz)	75g (2¾oz)
Black treacle (blackstrap molasses) (tbsp)	½	¾	1	1½	1½	1¾	2	2½	3
Baking time (hours)	2½	2¾	3	3½	4	4½	4¾	5½	6

Fillings and Coverings

Cakes are filled to give them extra flavour and moisture, and the choice of filling should complement the type or flavour of the sponge. The most popular and versatile fillings are buttercream and ganache. These recipes can be safely used on cakes displayed at room temperature, avoiding the need to refrigerate them until ready to serve. The fillings are also used to seal and coat the cake, filling in any gaps, correcting any imperfections and creating a firm, smooth surface for the icing.

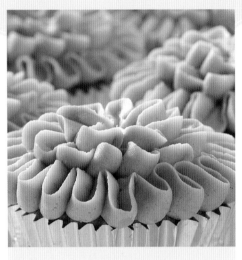

Makes about 500g (1lb 2oz), enough for an 18–20cm (7–8in) round or square layered cake or 20–24 cupcakes

Buttercream

Materials
170g (6oz) unsalted or slightly salted butter, softened

340g (12oz) icing (confectioners') sugar

2 tablespoons water

1 teaspoon vanilla extract or alternative flavouring (see Flavour Variations)

Equipment
Large electric mixer

Spatula

Put the butter and sugar in the bowl of a large electric mixer and mix together, starting on a low speed to prevent the mixture from going everywhere. Add the water and vanilla or other flavouring and increase the speed, beating the buttercream really well until it is pale, light and fluffy. Store for up to 2 weeks in an airtight container in the fridge.

Swiss meringue buttercream

Materials
140g (5oz) egg whites

200g (7oz) caster (superfine) or granulated sugar

Pinch of salt

454g (1lb) unsalted or slightly salted butter, very thoroughly softened until almost creamy

Equipment
Mixing bowl

Saucepan

Hand whisk

Large electric mixer with whisk attachment

This is lighter in taste and texture than regular buttercream, but it ideally needs to be used straight away and will last only a few hours out of the fridge. Filled cakes and macaroons can be refrigerated but should be eaten within 2 days.

One Put the egg whites, sugar and salt in a mixing bowl and set over a saucepan filled one-third to halfway with water (the water should touch the base of the bowl). Warm the mixture, stirring (not whisking) constantly with a hand whisk, until it reaches about 60°C (140°F) or until you can no longer feel the granules when you rub the mixture between your fingers.

Two Quickly transfer it to a large electric mixer fitted with a whisk attachment and whisk at high speed until a shiny meringue is formed and is very slightly warm to the touch. Reduce the mixer speed to low medium–low. Pinch off small chunks of butter and add one by one to the mixer bowl. When most of the butter has been incorporated the mixture will look like it has separated, but just continue whisking in the rest and it will finally come together.

Makes about 500g (1lb 2oz), enough for an 18–20cm (7–8in) round or square layered cake or 20–24 cupcakes

Ganache

Made from equal quantities of chocolate and cream, this luxurious filling is silky smooth and rich. Always buy good-quality chocolate for ganache with a cocoa solids content of at least 53 per cent. Ganache is also used for making cake pops to bind crumbled sponge together for rolling into balls (see Cake Pops).

Materials	Equipment
250g (9oz) plain (semisweet or bittersweet) chocolate, chopped, or callets	Saucepan
	Mixing bowl
250g (9oz) double (heavy) cream	Spatula

Put the chocolate in a bowl. Bring the cream to the boil in a saucepan, then pour over the chocolate. Stir until the chocolate has all melted and is perfectly combined with the cream. Leave to cool and then cover and store in the fridge. It will keep refrigerated for up to 1 week.

White chocolate ganache

Another sumptuous filling, this makes an ideal alternative to buttercream for using to fill heavy sponge cakes – that is, those that have been made with extra flour. Simply follow the Ganache recipe but use the same quantity of white chocolate in place of the plain (semisweet or bittersweet) chocolate and half the amount of cream. If you are making a small batch, melt the white chocolate before mixing it with the hot cream.

Sugar syrup

Brush onto the sponge to enhance its flavour and moistness. Use according to its taste or texture, but too much will make it overly sweet and sticky.

Materials	Equipment
85g (3oz) caster (superfine) sugar	Saucepan
80ml (2¾fl oz) water	Metal spoon
1 tsp vanilla extract (optional)	

Makes enough for a 20cm (8in) layered round cake (a square cake will need slightly more), 25 fondant fancies or 20–24 cupcakes

Bring the sugar and water to the boil, stirring once or twice. Add the vanilla extract, if using, and leave to cool. Store in an airtight container in the fridge for up to 1 month.

LEMON OR ORANGE FLAVOUR Replace the water with freshly squeezed, finely strained lemon or orange juice. You can also add a little lemon- or orange-flavoured liqueur (to taste) as well to heighten the citrusy taste.

Layering, filling and preparation

To achieve a professional-looking smooth and neatly shaped cake, preparing the cake in the right way ready for icing is essential. Sponge cakes usually consist of two or three layers (see Classic Sponge Cake), while fruit cakes are kept whole (see Traditional Fruit Cake).

Materials

Buttercream or ganache (see Fillings and
  Coverings), for filling and covering

Sugar syrup (see Fillings and Coverings),
  for brushing

Jam or conserve (preserves), for filling (optional)

Equipment

Cake leveller

Large serrated knife

Ruler

Small sharp paring knife (optional)

Cake board, plus chopping board or large cake
  board if needed

Turntable

Palette knives

Pastry brush

One Cut the dark-baked crust from the base of your cakes. If you have two sponges of equal depths, use a cake leveller to cut them to the same height. If you have baked one-third of your cake mixture in one tin and two-thirds in the other, cut two layers from the deeper sponge with a large serrated knife or cake leveller to make three layers. Alternatively, cut three layers from a larger square cake: cut a round from two opposite quarters of the square close to the corners for two layers, then a semicircle from the other two opposite quarters and piece together for the third layer. Your finished cake will be on a 1.25cm (½in) cake board, so the height of your layers together should be about 9cm (3½in) deep.

Two You should have either baked your cake 2.5cm (1in) larger all round than required or baked a larger sponge (see Classic Sponge Cake). Cut around your cake board (this will be the size of your cake), cutting straight down without angling the knife inwards or outwards. For round cakes, use a small sharp paring knife to do this and for square cakes use a large serrated one.

Be careful not to add too much filling between the sponge layers, as the cake will sink slightly under the weight of the icing and ridges will appear.

Three Place your three layers of sponge together to check that they are all even and level, trimming away any sponge if necessary. Place your base cake board on a turntable. If the board is smaller than the turntable, put a chopping board or another large cake board underneath. Use a non-slip mat if necessary.

Four Using a medium-size palette knife, spread a small amount of buttercream or ganache onto the cake board and stick down your bottom layer of sponge. Brush sugar syrup over the cake – the quantity depends on how moist you want your cake to be.

Five Spread an even layer of buttercream or ganache about 3mm (1/8in) thick over the sponge, then a thin layer of jam or conserve, if using any. Repeat this procedure for the next layer. Finish by adding the top layer and brushing with more sugar syrup.

Six Cover the side of the cake in buttercream or ganache, then the top – you only need a very thin and even layer. If the coating becomes 'grainy' as it picks up cake crumbs, place in the fridge for about 15 minutes to set and then add a thin second coat. This undercoat is referred to as a 'crumb coat' and helps to seal the sponge.

Seven Refrigerate your prepared cake for at least 1 hour so that it's firm before attempting to cover it with icing or marzipan; larger cakes will need chilling a little longer.

Filling and covering quantities

size	10cm (4in)	13cm (5in)	15cm (6in) 8–9 cupcakes	18cm (7in)	20cm (8in)	23cm (9in)	25cm (10in)	28cm (11in)
Buttercream or ganache	175g (6oz)	250g (9oz)	350g (12oz)	500g (1lb 2oz)	650g (1lb 7oz)	800g (1lb 12oz)	1.1kg (2lb 7oz)	1.25kg (2lb 12oz)

Covering with marzipan and sugarpaste

Before icing, your cake should be covered with a smooth layer of buttercream or ganache (see Layering, Filling and Preparation) to ensure that any irregularities or imperfections have been concealed or corrected, otherwise they will be visible through the icing. You can cover cakes with a second coat of icing if necessary, or cover with a layer of marzipan before you ice it with sugarpaste (rolled fondant).

Materials
Marzipan (optional)

Sugarpaste (rolled fondant)

Icing (confectioners') sugar, for dusting (optional)

Equipment
Greaseproof (wax) paper or baking (parchment) paper

Scissors

Large non-stick rolling pin

Large non-stick board with non-slip mat (optional)

Icing and marzipan spacers

Needle scriber

Icing smoother

Small sharp knife

Round cakes

One Cut a piece of greaseproof or baking paper about 7.5cm (3in) larger all round than your cake and put the cake on top.

Two Knead your marzipan or sugarpaste until soft. Roll it out with a large non-stick rolling pin on a large non-stick board, which usually won't need dusting with icing sugar, set over a non-stick mat. Otherwise, just use a work surface dusted with icing sugar. Use the spacers to give you the correct width – about 5mm (3/16in). Lift the sugarpaste up with the rolling pin to release it from the board and turn it a quarter turn before laying it back down to roll again. Try to keep it a round shape so that it will fit over your cake easily. Push out any air bubbles that may occur or use a needle scriber to burst them carefully.

Three Pick the sugarpaste up on your rolling pin and lay it over your cake. Quickly but carefully use your hands to smooth it around and down the side of the cake. Pull the sugarpaste away from the side of the cake as you go until you reach the base.

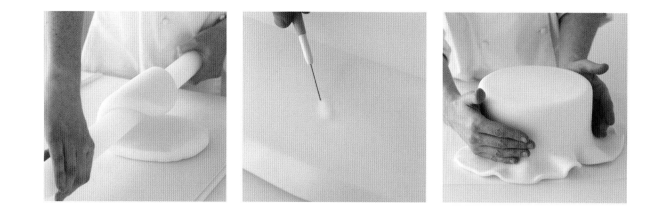

You need to work quite quickly with sugarpaste, as it will soon start to dry out and crack. Keep any leftover icing well wrapped in a plastic bag to prevent it from drying out.

Four When the icing is on, use a smoother in a circular motion to go over the top of the cake. For the side of the cake, work around the cake in forward circular movements, almost cutting the excess paste at the base. Trim the excess with a small sharp knife. Use the smoother to go around the cake one final time to make sure that it's perfectly smooth.

Square cakes

Icing a square cake is done in much the same way as a round cake, but take extra care with the corners to prevent the icing from tearing. Gently cup the icing in your hands around the corners before you start working it down the sides of the cake. Any tears in the icing can be mended with clean soft icing, but do this as soon as possible so that it blends in well.

Cake covering quantities

Cake size (9cm/3½in deep)	15cm (6in)	18cm (7in)	20cm (8in)	23cm (9in)	25cm (10in)	28cm (11in)
Marzipan/sugarpaste (rolled fondant)	650g (1lb 7oz)	750g (1lb 10oz)	850g (1lb 14oz)	1kg (2lb 4oz)	1.25kg (2lb 12oz)	1.5kg (3lb 5oz)

Allow slightly more for square cakes

Securing ribbon around cakes and boards

To secure ribbon around the base of a cake, first measure how long the ribbon needs to be by wrapping it around the cake so that it overlaps by about 1cm (³⁄₈in). Trim to length with a sharp pair of scissors. Attach double-sided tape to either end of the ribbon on the same side. Stick one end directly in place onto the icing, then wrap the ribbon around the cake and stick the other end, overlapping, onto the first end. For square cakes, put the double-sided tape around each corner as well as a small piece in the centre of each side.

To complete the professional presentation of your cake, attach double-faced satin ribbon around the edge of the cake board in a matching or complementary colour. Use ribbon 1.5cm (⁵⁄₈in) wide and secure at intervals around the board with double-sided tape.

Icing cake boards and dummies

Covering the base cake board with icing makes a huge difference to the finished cake, giving it a clean, professional finish. By carefully choosing the right colour for the icing, the board can be incorporated into the design of the cake itself.

To ice cake dummies, brush a small amount of water onto the dummy to help the icing stick in place, then cover with sugarpaste (rolled fondant) in the same way as you would a real cake (see Covering with Marzipan and Sugarpaste).

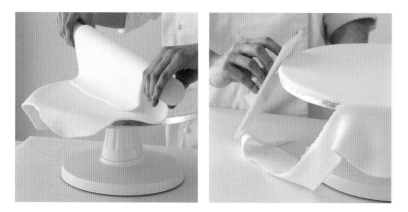

One Moisten the board with some water. Roll out the sugarpaste (rolled fondant) to 4mm (3/16in), ideally using icing or marzipan spacers. Place the board either on a turntable or bring it towards the edge of the work surface. Pick the icing up on the rolling pin and lay it over the cake board so that it is hanging down over it.

Two Use your icing smoother in a downwards motion to cut a smooth edge around the board. Cut away any excess icing. Finish by smoothing the top using circular movements to achieve a flat and perfectly smooth surface for your cake to sit on. Leave to dry overnight.

Cake board covering quantities

Cake board size	23cm (9in)	25cm (10in)	28cm (11in)	30cm (12in)	33cm (13in)	35.5cm (14in)
Sugarpaste (rolled fondant)	600g (1lb 5oz)	650g (1lb 7oz)	725g (1lb 9½oz)	850g (1lb 14oz)	1kg (2lb 4oz)	1.2kg (2lb 10½oz)

Assembling tiered cakes

When it comes to stacking cakes to create a series of tiers, you need to follow the correct procedure to ensure that the display has a dependable structure, but this is a straightforward process. I advise using hollow plastic dowels because of their sturdiness and the fact that they are easy to cut to the correct height. Thinner plastic dowels are suitable for smaller cakes. See the Dowels chart as a guide to the number of dowels you will need.

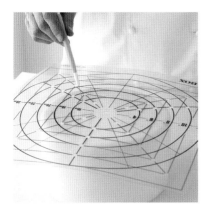

Materials
Iced cake board (see Icing Cake Boards
   and Dummies)
Stiff royal icing (see Royal Icing)

Equipment
Cake-top marking template
Needle scriber or marking tool
Hollow plastic dowels
Edible pen
Large serrated knife
Spare cake board
Spirit level
Icing smoothers

One Use the cake-top marking template to find the centre of your base cake.

Two Using a needle scriber or marking tool, mark the cake where the dowels should go. These need to be positioned well inside the diameter of the cake to be stacked on top. Push a dowel into the cake where it has been marked. Using an edible pen, mark the dowel where it meets the top of the cake.

Three Remove the dowel and cut it at the mark with a large serrated knife. Cut the other dowels to the same height and insert into the cake. Place a cake board on top of the dowels and check that they are equal in height by using a spirit level on the board.

Four Stick your base cake onto the centre of the iced cake board with stiff royal icing. Use your smoothers to move it into position if necessary. Leave the icing to set for a few minutes before stacking on the next tier. Repeat to attach a third tier if needed.

Dowel quantities

Cake size	15cm (6in)	20cm (8in)	25cm (10in)
No. of dowels	3–4	3–4	4–5

Mini cakes

You first need to bake a large square cake and then cut small round or square cakes from it. The number and size you want will determine the size of the large cake, but always opt for one slightly larger than your requirements to allow for wastage. I make my square mini cakes 5cm (2in), so for nine you will need an 18cm (7in) square cake. Refer to the charts in the Cake Recipes section, but use only two-thirds of the ingredient quantities, as mini cakes are shallower. Bake all the mixture in one tin (pan) rather than dividing it between two for larger cakes. Mini cakes are layered, filled and iced in a similar way to full-size cakes.

Materials

Large square baked classic sponge cake
   or classic chocolate cake
   (see Cake Recipes)

Sugar syrup (see Fillings and Coverings)

Buttercream or ganache (see Fillings
   and Coverings)

Sugarpaste (rolled fondant)

Equipment

Cake leveller

Circle cutter or serrated knife

Pastry brush

Cake card (optional)

Palette knife

Large non-stick rolling pin

Large non-stick board with non-slip mat

Metal ruler

Large sharp knife

Large circle cutter or small sharp knife

Two icing smoothers

One Slice your large square cake horizontally into two even layers using a cake leveller. Cut small individual rounds (using a cutter) or squares (using a serrated knife).

Two Brush the pieces of sponge with sugar syrup and sandwich together with either buttercream (plus jam if desired) or ganache if using a chocolate-flavoured cake. It's easier if you stick the bottom piece of cake to a cake card the same size and shape as your mini cake, using buttercream or ganache, but not essential. Working quickly, pick up each cake and cover the sides evenly with buttercream or ganache. Finish by covering the top and then place the cakes in the fridge for at least 20 minutes to firm up.

*It's much easier to work with the sponge if it's
very cold, as it will be a good deal firmer.*

Three Roll out a piece of sugarpaste 38cm (15in) square and 5mm (³/₁₆in) thick
with a large non-stick rolling pin on a large non-stick board set over a non-slip mat. Cut
nine small squares and lay one over each cake. If you are a beginner, prepare half the
cakes at a time, keeping the other squares under cling film (plastic wrap) to prevent them
drying out.

Four Use your hands to work the icing down around the sides of the cake and trim
away the excess with a large circle cutter, or small sharp knife if icing square cakes.

Five Use two icing smoothers on either side of the cake going forwards and
backwards and turning the cake as you go to create a perfectly smooth result. If icing
square cakes, use smoothers on opposite sides to press and smooth the icing around
the four sides. Leave the icing to dry, ideally overnight, before decorating the cakes.

*For mini traditional fruit cakes, bake the
mixture in small, individual tins, as they can't
be cut out due to the structure of the cakes.*

Baking cupcakes

The cake mixtures used for baking cupcakes are the same as those used for full-size cakes, and you can choose from classic sponge cake, classic chocolate cake or carrot cake (see Cake Recipes). For 10-12 cupcakes, use the quantities given for a 13cm (5in) round or 10cm (4in) square cake.

To bake the mixture, place cupcake cases (liners) in tartlet tins (pans) or muffin trays (pans) and fill them two-thirds to three-quarters full. Bake in a preheated oven at 180°C/350°F/Gas Mark 4 for about 20 minutes until springy to the touch.
I like to use plain foil cupcake cases (liners), available in a range of colours, because the foil keeps the cakes fresh and there is no pattern to draw attention away from the decoration on the cakes. But they also come in plain or patterned paper, and you can use decorative cases for plainer cupcakes.

Preparing and icing cupcakes

The cupcakes in this book have all been very simply iced with buttercream or ganache, which means that the cakes themselves don't need to be perfectly shaped, as the icing will hide any imperfections.

Before you prepare or ice the cupcakes, make sure they are completely cool. Brush the tops with extra sugar syrup if you think they might be a bit dry or if you want them to be really moist (see Fillings and Coverings). You can also 'inject' jams or conserves (preserves) into your sponge before you top them with buttercream or ganache. Simply fill a squeezy bottle with a narrow-pointed nozzle with the jam or conserve, carefully insert it into the cupcakes and squeeze.

To pipe your cupcakes, fit a large disposable plastic piping (pastry) bag with a large plain or star-shaped tube (tip), fill with buttercream or ganache (see Fillings and Coverings) and pipe a kiss (peak) or swirl onto the top – it will take a little practice to get each cake looking perfect. Alternatively, simply use a palette knife to spread the buttercream or ganache on evenly to create a neat domed top. Make sure your icing is soft when you use it – you may need to re-beat it or even warm it slightly if the room temperature is fairly cold.

Baking cookies

Suitable for almost every occasion, cookies also give you plenty of creative scope, as you can cut all manner of shapes from the dough and decorate them in many different ways. They offer an ideal opportunity to involve children in their preparation. Cookies can be made well in advance of the event for added convenience.

Makes 10–15 large or 25–30 medium

Flavour variations

CHOCOLATE Substitute 50g (1¾oz) flour with (unsweetened) cocoa.
CITRUS Omit the vanilla and add the finely grated zest of 1 lemon or orange.
ALMOND Replace the vanilla with 1 teaspoon almond extract.

Materials
250g (9oz) unsalted butter

250g (9oz) caster (superfine) sugar

1–2 medium eggs

1 tsp (5ml) vanilla extract

500g (1lb 2oz) plain (all-purpose) flour, plus extra for dusting

Equipment
Large electric mixer

Spatula

Deep tray or plastic container

Rolling pin

Cookie cutters or templates

Sharp knife (if using templates)

Baking trays (sheets) lined with greaseproof (wax) paper or baking (parchment) paper

Shelf life
The cookie dough can be made a few days ahead or stored in the freezer until ready to use. The baked cookies will keep for up to 1 month.

One In a large electric mixer, beat the butter and sugar together until creamy and quite fluffy.

Two Add the eggs and vanilla and mix until they are well combined.

Three Sift the flour, add to the bowl of the mixer and mix until all the ingredients just come together. You may need to do this in two stages – don't overmix.

Four Tip the dough into a container lined with cling film (plastic wrap) and press down firmly. Cover with cling film and refrigerate for at least 30 minutes.

Five On a work surface lightly dusted with flour, roll out the cookie dough to about 4mm (³/₁₆in) thick. Sprinkle a little extra flour on top of the dough as you roll to prevent it from sticking to the rolling pin.

Six Cut out your shapes either with cutters or using templates and a sharp knife. Place on baking trays lined with greaseproof or baking paper and return to the fridge to rest for at least 30 minutes. Meanwhile, preheat your oven to 180°C/350°F/Gas Mark 4.

Seven Bake the cookies for about 10 minutes, depending on their size, or until they are golden brown. Leave them to cool completely before storing them in an airtight container until you are ready to decorate them.

Fondant fancies

Try making these cute little cakes as an alternative to cupcakes. They can be a variety of shapes, the easiest being a square, cut from a large, shallow square or rectangular classic sponge cake in the same way as mini cakes (see Mini Cakes). If you want them to fit into a cupcake case (liner), make them about 4cm (1½in) square and 4cm (1½in) high - trim the top and bottom of the baked shallow cake to give you the correct height. The best flavours for the sponge are vanilla, lemon or orange.

Makes 16

Materials

25cm (10in) square shallow classic sponge cake (see Classic Sponge Cake, but use half the quantities specified), split into two layers and filled with jam, marmalade or lemon, lime or orange curd (see Layering, Filling and Preparation)

1 quantity sugar syrup, flavoured to match the sponge, and 1 quantity unflavoured (see Fillings and Coverings)

2 tablespoons apricot masking spread or strained jam, boiled and slightly cooled

225g (8oz) marzipan or sugarpaste (rolled fondant)

1.5kg (3lb 5oz) ready-made fondant

1 tbsp (15ml) liquid glucose

Food colouring, as required

Equipment

Pastry brush

Large non-stick rolling pin

Large non-stick board with non-slip mat

Icing or marzipan spacers

Icing smoothers

Metal ruler

Large and small sharp knife

Dipping fork

Wire rack

16 cupcake cases (liners)

One Once you have layered, filled and stuck the sponge back together, brush the remaining flavoured sugar syrup over the top of the sponge before covering it with a thin layer of the apricot masking spread or jam.

Two Roll the marzipan or sugarpaste out with a large non-stick rolling pin on a large non-stick board set over a non-slip mat to 3–4mm (⅛in) thick, using the spacers to guide you. Lay it over your sponge and run the smoother over the top so that it's firmly stuck down. Mark and cut 4cm (1½in) squares with a sharp knife, keeping the squares together until you are ready to dip them. Place the sponge in the fridge and chill for at least 1 hour.

Three Put the fondant in a microwave-proof bowl and warm in the microwave for about 1½ minutes on medium power until it can be easily poured.

Four Add the glucose and three-quarters of the unflavoured sugar syrup and gently stir together, trying to avoid introducing too many air bubbles. Add any food colouring. If you are not using immediately, cover the bowl with cling film (plastic wrap).

Five Return the fondant to the microwave and heat it gently until slightly warmer than body temperature (39–40°C/102–104°F). Test the consistency by dipping one of the fancies into the fondant. If it's too thick, add the remaining unflavoured sugar syrup until the fondant coats the cake well. Be careful not make it too runny or the fondant won't set.

Six Cut away any excess trimmings from the sponge. Plunge each square fancy, marzipan/icing side down, into your warm fondant. Working quickly, use the dipping fork to turn the fancy back upwards and move it across to the wire rack to allow the excess icing to drip down and off the sides of the cake. Repeat for each fancy.

Seven Remove the fancies from the rack, using a small sharp knife to cut away any excess fondant.

Eight Place each fancy into a cupcake case that has been slightly pressed out in advance so that the cake fits easily inside. Cup the case back up around the sides of the cake so that it takes on its shape. Place the fancies together, side by side, until they are completely set and ready to decorate, unless the decoration has been added beforehand so that it sticks in place as the fondant dries.

Cake pops

No wonder cake pops have become amazingly popular and fashionable in the last few years, as they are both fun and incredibly easy to make. They are made by rolling or shaping a chilled mixture of crumbled cake and ganache or buttercream into bite-size pieces, inserting lollipop sticks and dipping into chocolate or brightly coloured Candy Melts. You can bake a cake from scratch or use offcuts of cake left over from trimming cakes.

There are many ways that you can shape and decorate cake pops, but I like to keep mine very simple and scatter them with pretty sprinkles or chopped nuts. I also prefer to use chocolate cake mixed with ganache, although feel free to try any combination, such as lemon-flavoured sponge and white chocolate ganache.

Materials

Classic sponge cake or classic chocolate
    cake (see Cake Recipes)

Ganache or buttercream (see Fillings and
    Coverings), at room temperature

Tempered chocolate (see Working with
    Chocolate) or Candy Melts

Sprinkles or other decorations (optional)

Equipment

Mixing bowls

Large spoon or spatula

Disposable gloves

Tray lined with baking (parchment) paper

Lollipop/cake pop sticks

One Crumble the cake sponge into a mixing bowl. Gradually add the ganache or buttercream, stirring between each addition, until the pieces of cake become slightly moist and start to bind together almost like a cookie dough. Chill the mixture in the fridge for about 30 minutes, depending on the size of the batch you are making, until firm.

Two Put on a pair of disposable gloves. Roll bite-size pieces of the mixture into balls and place them on a tray lined with baking paper. Place them back in the fridge until you are ready to dip them – you don't want the cake pops to be really cold, just chilled enough so that they don't fall off the sticks when you dip them.

*To help make all your cake pops the same size,
weigh out the pieces of mixture before rolling them
– I make mine about 35g (1¹/₄oz) each.*

Three Prepare the Candy Melts according to the instructions on the packet or temper the chocolate (see Working with Chocolate).

Four Dip the very end of a lollipop stick/cake pop stick into the melted Candy Melts or chocolate, then push it straight into a cake pop. Use your thumb to remove the excess coating around the stick. Repeat for all the cake pops.

Five Dip the cake pops one at a time into the melted Candy Melts or chocolate. Twist them so that the entire ball is completely coated. Lift them out and remove the excess coating by gently shaking or tapping the sticks on the side of the bowl. Place them on the tray lined with baking paper. If you are decorating them with sprinkles or other decorations, scatter them over immediately before the coating sets.

Shelf life
Cake pops should be eaten within 2–3 days.

Meringues

These feather-light confections are a really useful addition to the sweet table, as they can be made in large quantities at low cost. The meringue mix is also easy to colour all kinds of pretty shades to suit your colour scheme and can be piped into a variety of decorative shapes, such as swirls and squiggles.

Makes 30–40 ping-pong ball-size pieces

Materials
600g (1lb 5oz) caster (superfine) sugar
150g (5½oz) water
225g (8oz) egg whites at room
   temperature
Food colouring

Equipment
Saucepan
Sugar (candy) thermometer
Large electric mixer with whisk
   attachment
Pastry brush
Large spatula
Two metal dessertspoons or large
   disposable plastic piping (pastry) bag
   and piping tube (tip)
Baking trays (sheets) lined with silicone
   sheets

One Preheat your oven to 75°C–110°F/170–225°F/Gas Mark ¼. Put the sugar and water in a saucepan and heat to 115°C (240°F) on a sugar thermometer.

Two Once the liquid in the pan has started to boil, start whisking the egg whites in a large electric mixer fitted with a whisk attachment on a medium speed so that soft peaks start to form.

Three As soon as the hot syrup has reached the correct temperature, steadily pour it into the whipped egg whites with the mixer still on, taking care not to splatter it around the bowl (see Macaroons). Keep the mixer on until the whites have cooled down almost to room temperature and you have a smooth, shiny mixture. If you are adding food colouring to the mix, add it towards the end of mixing.

Four Spoon or pipe the meringue mix onto baking trays lined with silicone sheets and bake for 30 minutes–1 hour depending on their size. The meringues are ready when you can lift them off the trays and if you tap them gently on the bottom they won't break.

Shelf life
The baked meringues can be stored for up to 2 weeks in an airtight container.

Brush the sides of the pan with water if the sugar starts to crystallize.

Macaroons

Macaroons are light and crispy baked confections rather like small cakes or meringue-like cookies and consist largely of ground almonds, similar to Italian amaretti. To make them, I prefer to use the Italian meringue method of pouring hot sugar syrup onto the whipped egg whites (see Meringues) because it tends to make a stiffer mixture, which is easier to work with. Various factors can affect the end results, such as humid conditions and in particular how your oven performs, so be prepared to experiment and persevere if your macaroons aren't quite right at the first attempt.

Materials

480g (1lb 1oz) ground almonds
480g (1lb 1oz) icing (confectioners')
   sugar
360g (12½oz) egg whites, at room
   temperature
480g (1lb 1oz) caster (superfine) sugar
120g (4¼oz) water
Food colouring
Swiss meringue buttercream,
   buttercream or ganache (see Fillings
   and Coverings), for filling

Equipment

Sieve (strainer)
Large mixing bowl
Large electric mixer with whisk
   attachment
Saucepan
Sugar (candy) thermometer
Large spatula
Pastry brush
Large and medium disposable plastic
   piping (pastry) bag
8mm (³/8in) piping tube (tip)
Baking trays (sheets) lined with silicone
   sheets

One Sift the ground almonds and icing sugar together into a large mixing bowl until you have a fine powder – you may need to sift the mixture twice.

Pulse the almond and sugar mixture in a food processor if the texture isn't fine enough.

Two Put half (180g/6¼oz) of the egg whites in the bowl of a large electric mixer fitted with a whisk attachment and whisk on a medium speed until you have soft peaks.

Three Meanwhile, put the caster sugar and water in a saucepan and heat to 115°C (240°F) on a sugar thermometer. Steadily pour it into the egg whites with the mixer still on, taking care not to splatter it around the bowl. Keep the mixer on until the whites have cooled down almost to room temperature and you have a smooth, shiny mixture.

Four Pour the remaining unused egg whites onto the almond/sugar powder and stir briefly before gently tipping in half of the meringue mixture.

Five Start folding the mixture together in a circular figure-of-eight motion carefully but fairly quickly using a large spatula and then add the rest of the meringue. It's better to slightly undermix at this stage because now is the time to add the food colouring. Do this gradually, using a clean knife or spatula, until you have the colour you require. The peaks in the mixture should have now disappeared and the surface should be glossy and smooth.

Six Spoon the mixture into a large plastic piping bag fitted with an 8mm (³/8in) piping tube. Pipe evenly shaped 3.5cm (1³/8in) discs onto baking trays lined with silicone sheets at least 3–4cm (1½in) apart. Leave for at least 20 minutes to allow the uncooked macaroons to dry out and form a skin. Meanwhile, preheat your oven to 150°C/300°F/Gas Mark 2.

Seven Bake the macaroons in the centre of the oven, one tray at a time, for 10–12 minutes. After about 6 minutes the macaroons will lift up and little 'feet' will appear. Turn the tray around if they look like they are baking unevenly. The macaroons are ready when they are just firm to the touch on top.

Eight Remove the macaroons from the oven and leave to cool on a wire rack for a few minutes. Remove the macaroons from the baking trays by carefully twisting them off or running a small sharp knife underneath them. Set them aside or store in an airtight container until required.

Nine Fill a medium disposable plastic piping bag with Swiss meringue buttercream, buttercream or ganache, either fitted with the 8mm (³/8in) piping tube or snip off the end of the bag, and use to sandwich the baked macaroon shells together.

Shelf life

The filled macaroons can be stored for up to 2–3 days. You can keep them in the fridge to help them stay fresher for a day or so longer. The unfilled macaroon shells can be kept for up to 2 months in the freezer.

Royal icing

Learning to work with royal icing is a key skill in cake decorating. Royal icing is such a versatile medium, used for icing cakes and cookies, intricate piping of decorations or simply attaching and sticking.

It's best to use royal icing while it's as fresh as possible, but it will keep for up to 5 days in an airtight container. If not used straight away, re-beat the icing back to its correct consistency before using.

Materials
2 medium egg whites or 15g (½oz) dried
egg albumen powder mixed with 75ml
(2½fl oz) water
500g (1lb 2oz) icing (confectioners')
sugar

Equipment
Large electric mixer
Sieve (strainer)
Spatula

One If using dried egg powder, soak it in the water for at least 30 minutes in advance, but ideally overnight in the fridge.

Two Sift the icing sugar into the bowl of a large electric mixer and add the egg whites or strained reconstituted egg mixture.

Three Mix together on a low speed for about 3–4 minutes until the icing has reached a stiff-peak consistency, which is what you need for sticking on decorations and gluing cakes together.

Four Store the icing in an airtight container covered with a damp, clean cloth to prevent it from drying out.

Soft-peak royal icing

To pipe decorations easily, you may need to add a tiny amount of water to your royal icing to soften it slightly.

Run-out icing

Royal icing is thinned down with water to 'flood' cookies (see Royal-Iced Cookies). Test for consistency by lifting your spoon and letting the icing drip back into the bowl – it should remain on the surface for 5 seconds before disappearing. If it's too runny it will run over the outlines and sides of the cookies, but if it's too stiff it won't spread very well.

Making a piping bag

One Cut two equal triangles from a large square of greaseproof (wax) paper or baking (parchment) paper. As a guide, for small piping (pastry) bags cut from a 15–20cm (6–8in) square and for large bags cut from a 30–35.5cm (12–14in) square.

Two If right-handed, keeping the centre point towards you with the longest side farthest away, curl the right-hand corner inwards and bring the point to meet the centre point. Adjust your hold so the two points are together between right thumb and index finger.

Three With your left hand, curl the left point inwards, bringing it across the front and around to the back of the other two points in the centre of the cone. Adjust your grip so that you are holding the three points together with both thumbs and index fingers. Tighten the cone by gently rubbing your thumb and index fingers forwards and backwards until you have a sharp tip at the end of the bag.

Four Carefully fold the back of the bag (where all the points meet) inwards and press hard along the fold. Repeat to secure.

Piping with royal icing

For basic piping work, use soft-peak royal icing (see Royal Icing). The size of the tube (tip) you use will depend on the job at hand and how competent you are.

Fill the piping (pastry) bag until it's no more than one-third full. Fold the top over, away from the join, until you have a tight and well-sealed bag. The correct way to hold the piping bag is important. Use your index finger to guide the bag. You can also use your other hand to guide you if it's easier.

To pipe dots, squeeze the icing out gently until you have the dot that's the size you want. Stop squeezing, then lift the bag. If there is a peak in the icing, use a damp brush to flatten it down.

To pipes lines, touch the tube down, then lift the bag up in a smooth movement, squeezing gently. Decrease the pressure and touch it back down to the point where you want the line to finish. Try not to drag the icing along, or it will become uneven. Use a template or a cookie outline as a guide where possible.

Royal-iced cookies

This is my favourite method of icing cookies, as I love the taste of the crisp white icing against the softer texture of the cookie underneath. Most of the cookie projects in this book have been iced this way. If you are icing a large quantity of cookies, use a squeezable plastic bottle with a small tube (tip) instead of piping (pastry) bags.

Materials
Soft-peak royal icing (see Royal Icing)

Equipment
Small and large paper piping (pastry) bags
 (see Making a Piping Bag)
Piping tubes (tips) nos. 1.5 or 2 and 1

One Place the no. 1.5 or 2 tube in a small paper piping bag and fill with some soft-peak royal icing. Pipe an outline around the edge of each cookie.

Two Thin down some more royal icing with water until 'flooding' consistency (see Run-Out Icing) and place in a large paper piping bag fitted with a no. 1 tube. Use to flood inside the outlines on the cookies with icing. For larger cookies, you can snip off the end of the bag instead of using a tube. If the area you need to flood is relatively large, work around the edges of the piped outline and then inwards to the centre to ensure an even covering.

Three Once dry, pipe over any details that are required and stick on any decorations.

Covering cookies with sugarpaste

For a very simple and speedy way to ice cookies that looks neat and professional, roll out some sugarpaste (rolled fondant) to no more than 3mm (1/8in) thick and cut out the shape of the cookie with the same cutter or template used for cutting out the cookies from the cookie dough. Stick the cut-out icing shapes onto the cookies using boiled and cooled apricot masking spread or strained jam, taking care not to stretch and distort the icing.

Working with flower paste

When you want to create delicate icing decorations for cakes and cookies, such as flowers, frills and bows, flower (petal/gum) paste is the most successful medium because it can be rolled out really thinly. Before using the paste, knead it thoroughly by continuously pulling it apart with your fingers.

Modelling paste and CMC

Similar to sugarpaste (rolled fondant) only stiffer in consistency, modelling paste is used for moulding more robust shapes and decorations. It doesn't dry out as quickly as flower (petal/gum) paste yet neither has it the same strength. You can buy modelling paste ready-made, but it's cost-effective and very easy to make your own using CMC (sodium carboxymethyl cellulose), which comes in the form of a powder that you knead into sugarpaste. As a guide, use about 1 teaspoon per 300g (10½oz) icing.

Colouring icings

Three kinds of food colouring are used to colour icing: paste, liquid and less commonly powder. I prefer paste for colouring sugarpaste (rolled fondant), flower (petal/gum) paste and marzipan because it doesn't make the icing wet and sticky. Add small amounts with a cocktail stick (toothpick) and larger amounts with a knife, then knead it into the icing. Always add colouring gradually and keep some extra white icing to hand in case you add too much. Liquid food colour is good for colouring royal icing and liquid fondant, but be careful not to add too much too soon. Be aware that the colour of icing can change as it dries – some colours tend to fade while others darken.

It's best to colour more icing than you need to allow for mishaps. Any leftovers can be stored in an airtight bag in a sealed container.

Working with chocolate

When melting chocolate for decorating cakes and other confections, you need to temper it to keep it looking lovely and glossy rather than developing a 'bloom' – a matt finish with white/grey areas and a crumbly texture caused by uneven crystallization of the cocoa butter. Tempering involves the controlled heating and cooling of the chocolate and can be done in various ways, but this microwave method is the quickest and easiest.

Materials
500g (1lb 2oz) plain (semisweet or bittersweet) couverture chocolate callets (about 53% cocoa solids)

Equipment
Microwave-proof plastic mixing bowl
Microwave

To temper the chocolate, put the chocolate callets into a microwave-proof plastic mixing bowl. Place the bowl in the microwave and gradually melt the chocolate on medium-high power, stirring it every 15–20 seconds so that the heat is evenly distributed with no 'hot spots'. When the chocolate has nearly all melted but there are still a few small pieces in the bowl, remove from the microwave and stir until the remaining pieces have melted. The chocolate is now ready to use.

*For the **Chocolate-Wrapped Rose Raptures** (see A Feast of Roses), first pieces of acetate are smeared with tempered chocolate using a cranked palette knife so that it runs completely over all the edges.*

*For the **Romancing Raspberry Truffles** (see A Feast of Roses), ganache is piped into hollow truffle shells and then the shells are sealed with tempered chocolate to fill them completely without leaving any air pockets.*

Each truffle in turn is then dipped into the bowl of tempered chocolate with a dipping fork, lifted out and the excess chocolate allowed to drip off before transferring to a sheet of baking (parchment) paper. They are sprinkled with crystallized raspberries to finish.

Before the chocolate has time to set, the acetate is wrapped around the mini cake with the chocolate side against the cake, allowing one end to very slightly overlap the other. The cakes are then placed in the fridge for a few minutes to set, then the acetate carefully removed.

Suppliers

UK

THE CAKE PARLOUR
146, Arthur Road, London,
SW19 8AQ
Tel: 020 8947 4424
www.thecakeparlour.com

THE CANDY CAN CO.
6 McDonald Road,
Longforgan,
Perthshire, DD2 5BW
Tel: 01382 360640
www.thecandycancompany.com

RUCRAFT
Brunel House
Newton Abbot
Devon, TQ12 4PU
www.rucraft.co.uk

SQUIRE'S KITCHEN SHOP
3 Waverley Lane, Farnham,
Surrey, GU9 8BB
Tel: 0845 6171810
www.squires-shop.com

THE SUGAR SHACK
Unit 12, Bowmans Trading Estate,
Westoreland Road,
London, NW9 9RL
Tel: 020 8204 2994
www.sugarshack.co.uk

US

CANDY.COM
Tel: 888-422-6393
www.candy.com

DESIGNER STENCILS
Designer Stencils, 2503 Silverside Road,
Wilmington, DE 19810
Tel: 800-822-7836
www.designerstencils.com

GLOBAL SUGAR ART
625 Route 3, Unit 3, Plattsburgh,
NY 12901
Tel: 1-518-561-3039
www.globalsugarart.com

Credits

The author and the publisher would like to thank the following:

AYRES AND GRACES
29A London Road,
Dunstable,
Beds, LU6 3DH
Tel: 01582 536760
www.ayersandgraces.com

CHANDOS HOUSE
2 Queen Anne Street,
London, W1G 9LQ
Tel: 020 7290 3860
www.chandoshouse.co.uk

DAVID AUSTIN ROSES
Bowling Green Lane,
Albrighton,
Wolverhampton, WV7 3HB
Tel: 01902 376300
www.davidaustinroses.com

NONSUCH MANSION
Nonsuch Park,
Ewell Road, Cheam
Surrey, SM3 8AL
Tel: 020 8786 8124
www.nonsuchmansion.com

PAPER MOON
The Studio, 3 Hill Road,
London, NW8 9QE
Tel: 020 7286 9455
www.papermoon.co.uk

PAPERPOMS UK
Tel: 07947 308325
www.paperpoms.co.uk

RAYNERS CATERING EQUIPMENT HIRE
Banquet House,
118–120 Garratt Lane,
London, SW18 4DJ
Tel: 020 8870 6000
www.rayners.co.uk

ROSANNA IMPORTS, INC.
6755 East Marginal Way S
Bldg B, Seattle,
WA 98108,
USA
Tel: 877-343-3779
www.rosannainc.com

STEPHANIE DYMENT
Amber House
2 Governors Close
Amersham
Bucks, HP6 6UP
Tel: 01494 581775
www.stephaniedyment.com

ZITA ELZE
287 Sandycombe Road,
Kew, Richmond,
Surrey, TW9 3LU
Tel: 020 8940 0040
www.zitaelze.com

About the author

Zoe Clark is one of London's leading cake designers, and her work regularly appears in the UK's bestselling bridal and sugarcraft magazines. Her cake designs have also featured on television and in films, and she has previously produced four books for D&C showcasing her unique style. Zoe opened The Cake Parlour in South West London in November 2010, where as well as offering a bespoke cake and confectionery design service for every occasion she also runs cake-decorating classes for aspiring cake decorators from all over the country and beyond. Zoe has recently started supplying the world-renowned Fortnum & Mason store with an exclusive range of wedding and celebration cakes and cookies.

www.thecakeparlour.com
www.zoeclarkcakes.com

Acknowledgments

It's been such a pleasure designing and creating the various sweet tables in this book, and I'm thrilled to have the opportunity to share them with a wider audience.

Firstly, I'd like to thank everyone at David and Charles for their help and for allowing me to produce this book. Much thanks to the amazingly talented Sarah Underhill for designing the beautiful pages and for helping me style all the sweet tables, and to Mark Scott for the wonderful photography – you've both been so much fun to work with. Thanks too to the lovely Jo Richardson for editing my text, and to everyone else who has contributed to the making of this book.

I would also like to thank the following for their invaluable input: Chandos House (Lullaby of Sweet Loves) and Nonsuch Mansion (A Romance of Ruffles and A Feast of Roses) for allowing us to shoot in their buildings; Zita Elze and David Austin Roses for the flowers used in A Romance of Ruffles and A Feast of Roses; Juliet of Paperpoms for the paper pompoms in A Romance of Ruffles; Rayners Catering Equipment Hire for the silverware in A Feast of Roses; Paper Moon for the delightful striped wallpaper in The Candy Collection; Ayres and Graces for the black frames and Rosanna Imports, Inc. for the black cake stands in At the Cake Parlour (see Credits for contact details).

Finally, thanks to my gorgeous children and loving husband and family for all their support and encouragement. I love you all.

Index

A DAVID & CHARLES BOOK
© F&W Media International, Ltd 2012

David & Charles is an imprint of F&W Media International, Ltd
Brunel House, Forde Close, Newton Abbot, TQ12 4PU, UK

F&W Media International, Ltd is a subsidiary of F+W Media, Inc
10151 Carver Road, Cincinnati OH45242, USA

Text and Designs © Zoe Clark 2012
Layout and Photography © F&W Media International, Ltd 2012

First published in the UK and USA in 2012

Zoe Clark has asserted her right to be identified as author of this work in
accordance with the Copyright, Designs and Patents Act, 1988.

A catalogue record for this book is available from the British Library.

ISBN-13: 978-1-4463-0200-2 paperback
ISBN-10: 1-4463-0200-8 paperback

Paperback edition printed in China by RR Donnelley for:
F&W Media International, Ltd
Brunel House, Forde Close, Newton Abbot, TQ12 4PU, UK

10 9 8 7 6 5 4 3 2 1

Acquisitions Editor: Katy Denny
Editor: James Brooks
Project Editor: Jo Richardson
Art Editor: Sarah Underhill
Photographer: Mark Scott
Senior Production Controller: Kelly Smith

F+W Media publishes high quality books on a wide range of subjects.
For more great book ideas visit: **www.rucraft.co.uk**